CW00505418

ACQUAINTED WI

An Exploration of Spirituality and Depression

Robert Waldron

ACQUAINTED WITH THE NIGHT

An Exploration of Spirituality and Depression

Robert Waldron

DARTON·LONGMAN+TODD

First published in 2012 by
Darton, Longman and Todd Ltd
1 Spencer Court
140 – 142 Wandsworth High Street
London SW18 4JJ

Copyright © 2012 Robert Waldron

The right of Robert Waldron to be identified as the author of this work has been asserted in accordance with the Copyright, Designs and Patents Act 1988.

ISBN: 978-0-232-52914-2

A catalogue record for this book is available from the British Library.

Phototypeset by Kerrypress Ltd, Luton, Beds.
Printed and bound in Great Britain by Bell & Bain, Glasgow

Dedicated to Margaret C. Waldron

Contents

Introduction

Depression is pandemic today; it has clawed its way even into the minds and souls of our young people, so that it is not unusual to hear that teenagers, or children, are taking antidepressants or even committing suicide. This book, however, will address alternative ways of coping with depression, not antidepressants and not therapy. We must, of course, accept that certain kinds of depression, for instance clinical depression, should be treated by the medical profession; and for long-term depression, which refuses to disappear, therapy may be required. We are more concerned with the kind of depression that most of us in our lives have experienced. Sometimes it can be of a short duration; at other times it stubbornly lingers while we helplessly stand and wait. The aim of this book is to illustrate that depression is often a spiritual malaise that can be 'treated' by spiritual measures; for example, embarking on the inner journey, seeking greater self-knowledge, and turning to God through prayer and contemplation.

In addressing depression and spirituality, I propose the usage of Carl Jung's theory of individuation. I choose to employ a Jungian perspective because Freud dismisses religion (spirituality) as neurosis while Jung claims that religion (spirituality) is its cure. According to Jung, depression, the kind the average person experiences, is the unconscious method of alerting us that all is not well within our inner lives.

A classic description of depression is found in Hamlet's account of himself to Rosencrantz and Guildenstern:

> I have of late, but wherefore I know not, lost all mirth, forgone all custom of exercises, and, indeed, it goes so heavily with my disposition that this goodly frame, the earth, seems to me a sterile promontory; this most excellent canopy, the air, look you, this brave o'er-hanging firmament, this majestical roof, fretted with golden fire – why, it appeareth nothing to me but a foul and pestilent congregation of vapors. What a piece of work is a man, how noble in reason, how infinite in faculties, in form and moving how express and admirable; in action how like an angel, in apprehension how like a god: the beauty of the world, the paragon of animals-and yet to me, what is this quintessence of dust? Man delights not me, nor women neither ... (*Hamlet* Act 2 scene 2)

A depressed person has no mirth, is blind to the beauty of earth and sky, everything seems 'pestilent' – diseased. We find in Hamlet's words an excellent example of psychological projection: the depressed, sad inner self is projected onto the world, and it is often projected onto people; thus, Hamlet takes no joy in other people, neither men nor women, every person dismissed as a 'quintessence of dust'. Hamlet's description of his psychic/spiritual soulscape correlates with Jung's description of depression:

> There are moments in human life when a new page is turned. New interests and tendencies appear which have hitherto received no atten-

tion, or there is a sudden change of personality (a so-called mutation of character). During the incubation period (depression) of such a change we can observe a loss of conscious energy: the new development has drawn off the energy it needs from consciousness.[1]

This book emphasises that depression is usually not pathological; in fact, it often foreshadows a renewal of the personality or a burst of creative activity. In Christian terms, a person is 'resurrected' by recognising and embracing 'not I, but Christ within me' (Gal. 2:20). If taken seriously, people with depression who are willing to listen to their inner self, or what Christians call the 'still, small voice of God', can transform their lives, and for Christians this transformation means not only more meaningful relationships with those people we love but also a closer, loving relationship with God, through prayer, faith, hope and love.

We will explore the common causes and symptoms of depression, and by so doing underscore the Socratic ideal: 'the unexamined life is not worth living'. When a person is depressed, the unconscious invites a person to embark upon an inner journey, for cure of depression lies in greater self-knowledge that allows an individual to attain greater wholeness in life. Jung considers wholeness as the goal of individuation. He describes the latter, 'A state in which consciousness and the unconscious work together in harmony … In terms of individuation, where the goal is a vital connection with the Self.' Jung states that for western men and women the archetypal Self is the Christ.

A Christian who seeks wholeness also seeks holiness. Much harm has been done with a mistransla-

tion of Christ's dictum, 'Be ye perfect as your
heavenly Father is perfect.' Too often Christians have
literally believed that they could achieve perfection
in this life. Such a goal invariably leads to frustration
and often to depression because no one is capable of
perfection; even our greatest saints remained flawed
human beings. Jung explains that the Greek word
commonly translated as 'perfect' is closer in meaning
to the words complete and whole.[2] As human beings,
we can indeed realistically reach for completeness
and wholeness by accepting ourselves, including
our imperfections. If a person is whole, he or she is
also holy because he or she has loved his or her own
personhood as Christ enjoins us to do: 'Love your
neighbour as you love yourself.' We cannot be holy if
we do not accept or love ourselves. The locus of love
resides within us.

When people with depression take their depression seriously, they see that they are living superfi-
cially and understand that there is a deeper kind of
living available: it is this realisation that leads them
into a spiritual dimension. They often turn to God,
out of desperation, of desolation, of a need for meaning; other times it is simply out of a need for self-
acceptance and love. Our God is one of agape: his
love is unconditional. Thus, this love alone can transform those suffering depression, many of whom are
people filled with self-loathing (often because they
tried to be 'perfect' and failed), filled with low self-
esteem, who daily chastise themselves, thus render-
ing their life a hell on earth, that is, a state of being
called depression.

The cure for much depression lies within the
Christian message of mercy, forgiveness, compassion, acceptance and love. Patrick Howell SJ, a priest
whose depression caused his nervous breakdown,
writes:

It takes a long time to believe that I am accepted by God as I am. How often have we
been told that it is important that we love God.
And this is true. But it is far more important
that God love us! We measure love. God does
not. God can only love totally, 100 percent ...
God's love is infinite, so we cannot grasp it,
narrow it down.[3]

All we can do is jump into it. And we do not like to
jump. We are afraid to let go. It is fairly easy to
believe in God's love for others. But why me? Few
people can really accept themselves, accept acceptance. Self-acceptance is an act of faith. When God
loves me, I must accept myself as well. I cannot be
more demanding than God, can I?

The radiant theme of this book is that cure for
much depression lies within our following and emu-
lating the example of Jesus Christ and his message of
Love.

Notes

1 Daryl Sharp, *Jung Lexicon: A Primer of Terms and
   Concepts* (Toronto: Inner City Books, 1991), p. 46.
2 *Selected Letters of C. G. Jung, 1909–1961*, ed.
   Gerhard Adler (Princeton: Princeton University
   Press, 1984), p. 140.
3 Patrick Howell SJ, *Reducing the Storm to a Whisper:
   The Story of a Breakdown* (Chicago: The Thomas
   More Press, 1985), p. 113.

1

The Affinity between Wholeness and Holiness

The focus in this book is the soul and the meaning of being truly whole and holy. For far too long wholeness and holiness have been divided, but there is no duality: to be whole is to be holy. How is this statement true? For Carl Jung wholeness is the fruit of the person who has taken his individuation seriously, his soul-making, which occurs when a person becomes centred not in the ego but in the archetypal Self, and for Jung the Self is Christ. Similarly, the Christian who seeks holiness is a person whose aim is unity with the Christ, one who can say with humility, 'Not I, but Christ within me.' Thus in both instances, Christ is the centre, the unifying force of the psyche/soul; therefore, there is no duality. When speaking about wholeness, we are not referring to perfection. Christians for generations have taken literally Christ's injunction, 'Be ye perfect as your heavenly father is perfect.' This translation has caused many a Christian anguish, if not agony. Jung wisely counselled a Dominican priest about his unsuccessful search for perfection, informing him that the word often translated from Greek as 'perfect' is really closer in meaning to complete or whole; thus, Christ's command to be perfect suffers a tremendous sea change, for attaining wholeness is something most people can indeed accomplish in life.[1]

Let it be noted that holiness is not something to be achieved; it is not a goal. Reciting a million rosaries, attending thousands of Masses, daily praying the Our Father will not render one holy. Everyone already possesses holiness within. Our most important work in life is to unveil this inner holiness by bringing it into sight so that we can behold it. Its sight will enlighten us, for as Plato reminds us, 'You become what you behold.' Rituals like the rosary, attendance at Mass and the saying of the Our Father are indeed important in our spiritual lives because they draw our gaze from our ego, thus freeing the unconscious to make contact with our conscious mind by offering it insights, intuitions, flashes of self-knowledge, dreams, hints and guesses, which if attentively pondered, yield gems of self-knowledge, unveiling the hidden holiness and wholeness that abides within us. Holiness, therefore, is not something we have to win, like an athlete training to win an Olympic medal. Holiness is not a prize, it is a state of being we possess, but it is indeed up to us to help what is dormant to begin to bloom with the sunlight of our attention and the rain of our tears. Depression, consequently, has a purpose, even though it brings pain into our lives. If heeded, however, depression can help us become self-realised, self-actuated and individuated human beings.

The question we should first address is, why are there today so many depressed people? It is almost impossible to answer such a question, but we will make an attempt to answer this question because we must seek knowledge, and when in the dark, we cannot resist searching for the light, as this idea also applies to our soul-making. The analogy of light is apropos: people who suffer from depression can be described as people who abide in darkness. The darkness comes to one as swiftly as a thief in the night, stealing one's energy, optimism, desires, hopes and dreams. The depressed person often does not really understand what hit her. What she knows is that she is not herself.

Thus, depression is an obstacle to our being and becoming ourselves. It is an obstacle to our soul's hunger and thirst for wholeness, which is also holiness. It is a state of being that does not come from outside of ourselves. Again, we are not addressing clinical depression, whose cause may be genetic or chemical. We are addressing the kind of depression most of us experience in our lives, some of a short duration, some chronic.

Where does depression reside? Within ourselves, in what Carl Jung has described as our unconscious mind. Why would the unconscious deliberately drag a man, woman or young adult down into depression? The unconscious mind is alerting a person that on some level he is not living fully. And depression is a way to stop a person in his tracks, to take his eyes from the external world and to look inward. James Hillman, the famous Jungian therapist, when asked to define depression, said, 'It is hidden knowledge.'

If a depressed person takes his or her depression seriously, refuses to run away from it and chooses to embark upon the inner journey, then he or she will indeed find the reason for that depression, and will find the true Self.

In the early twentieth century, many people turned to Freud to cure their neuroses often manifested by depression. Freud felt that if he could dig up through psychoanalysis a buried negative childhood memory, it would free his patient. He also theorised that the cause of neurosis was more often than not the result of repressed sexuality. Many modern people, especially those of the generation after the First World War, felt that if they freed themselves from all their inhibitions and led sexually liberated lives by openly and often expressing their sexuality, they would become healthy, happy people.

It took a generation to discover that repressed sexuality was not the root cause of the modern person's depression, unhappiness and sense of meaninglessness. Carl Jung broke with Freud over such a narrow view of life. He felt that the cause of depression was far more complicated than repressed sexuality. He theorised that human beings had lost touch with their souls, with God. Darwinian theory and the ravages of the First World War exerted a tremendously negative effect on modern men and women: without faith they had no anchor in life. But Freudian psychoanalysis proved wanting: it was not the promised cure to their soul's sickness, one so masterfully described in T. S. Eliot's poetry, particularly *The Waste Land*, and *The Hollow Men*.

The modern spiritual malaise began in 1850 with the publication of Charles Darwin's *The Origin of the Species*. His theory of evolution brought into doubt the truth of the Bible, with people beginning to question their religion and doubt their faith. Alfred Lord Tennyson had read Darwin and began to doubt the existence of God. To lose one's faith in God would cast anyone into depression, as it did Tennyson. Then when his dearest friend Arthur Hallam died, life seemed meaningless to him. But he fought to hold onto his religious faith. Reading his masterpiece *In Memoriam*, one encounters one of the world's greatest spiritual autobiographies. In the end Tennyson was able to win a beleaguered faith, one that remained with him to his death. But he was one of the lucky nineteenth-century poets. Other poets, however, lost their youthful faith. Thomas Hardy lost his faith, becoming a pessimist, his pessimism evident both in his verse and in his novels. Matthew Arnold became an agnostic. His poem 'Dover Beach' aptly describes what ailed so many of the late nineteenth century:

The Sea of Faith
Was once, too, at the full, and round earth's shore
Lay like the folds of a bright girdle furl'd.
But now I only hear
Its melancholy, long, withdrawing roar,
Retreating, to the breath
Of the night-wind, down the vast edges drear
And naked shingles of the world.

Ah, love, let us be true
To one another! for the world, which seems
To lie before us like a land of dreams,
So various, so beautiful, so new,
Hath really neither joy, nor love, nor light,
Nor certitude, nor peace, nor help for pain;
And we are here as on a darkling plain
Swept with confused alarms of struggle and flight,
Where ignorant armies clash by night.

Let us briefly look at the last two stanzas of Arnold's masterpiece. The sea of faith is no longer at the full; its withdrawing roar is described as one of 'melancholy'. This word 'melancholy' makes us sit up and pay attention. Melancholy can simply mean sad or mournful. And it is indeed sad for men and women to lose their faith because for many of them a life without faith is a meaningless life. But to lose one's faith can cause a person to become more than sad, to become depressed, a deeper, darker, more enervated state of soul. A depressed person finds no joy in life; in fact, many depressed people ponder suicide.

Without a living faith, and without religion, where does a person turn for sustenance? For Arnold, it is human love. Thus, he says to his beloved, 'Ah, love, let us/Be true to one another.' He does not believe in the supernatural, and he understands that he cannot rely on the natural, the world, one he describes in negative terms, one where there is no love, no light, no certitude, no help for inner pain. Then he offers his most harrowing epithet for the world, comparing it to a place of constant war, 'Where ignorant armies clash by night', a world caught in its own collective 'dark night of the soul'.

Needless to say, Arnold was a depressed man when he wrote 'Dover Beach', depressed because he longed to believe in God, but agnosticism had taken hold of him. While visiting France with his new wife, Arnold visited the famous abbey, the Grand Chartreuse, where he stayed overnight and attended the Midnight Mass. He was so moved by the event, he composed one of his most beautiful poems, 'Stanzas from the Grande Chartreuse', in which he expresses his spiritual dilemma:

> Wandering between two worlds, one dead,
> The other powerless to be born,
> With nowhere yet to rest my head,
> Like these, on earth I wait forlorn.
> Their faith, my tears, the world deride –
> I come to shed them at their side.
>
> Oh, hide me in your gloom profound,
> Ye solemn seats of holy pain!
> Take me, cowl'd forms, and fence me round,
> Till I possess my soul again;

Till free my thoughts before me roll,
Not chafed by hourly false control!

For the world cries your faith is now
But a dead time's exploded dream;
My melancholy, sciolists say,
Is a pass'd mode, an outworn theme –
As if the world had ever had
A faith, or sciolists been sad!

In his poem, he claims 'my melancholy'. He is a man
caught between two worlds, one dead and the other
powerless to be born. The world of universal faith is
dead, and as for the future, he is uncertain because he
does not know what can replace religion. For a time
he believes that art can replace it, but he knows it will
not be enough to cure his 'gloom profound'. It is
unfortunate that he did not live long enough to read
Carl Jung, as Jung would have convinced him that a
man does indeed have a soul and is happy when his
life is grounded in faith, in God. Arnold would need
to hear these words from his intellectual equal, a man
who could match him with intellectual brilliance.
Arnold may indeed possess a fine intellect, and he
may have, like many intellectuals of his day, been
impressed by the new knowledge of science (for
example, the work of Lyell and Huxley and the
theory of Charles Darwin), but the fact of the matter
is that Arnold has lost his soul: 'Till I possess my soul
again'. His usage of the word soul is proof enough of
his ambivalence. He is indeed caught between a rock
and a hard place: a part of him still believes in the
soul, but being a man of his time, he describes himself as an agnostic. Carl Jung says of agnosticism,
'Agnosticism is never sufficient when it comes to the
question of life as a whole. We need certain general

views about things we cannot know in order to sum
up our specific life experiences or to satisfy our
desire for self-cognition and wholeness.'[2] People
without faith are often prone to depression. Without
God in their lives, they assume that life has no meaning, one of the major causes of depression today.
People need to believe in something; consequently,
the great question with which every human being
must grapple is, 'Does God exist?'

And yet many people today are not articulating
this question, never mind answering it. Whereas the
repression of the sexual instinct was the dilemma of
people in the early part of the twentieth century,
today's unhealthy repression is that of the religious
impulse, one that every person possesses. One can
allow this impulse space in the conscious mind or
repress it into the unconscious mind. If repressed,
however, it does not disappear and manifests itself in
moods, mania, anxiety, insomnia, fear – in short,
depression.

The person who fails to address the Great Question ends up focusing on the ego. Such a person
avoids thinking of the eternal verities, the meaning
of life, the meaning of love, the meaning of forgiveness. Such a person does not have his 'act together',
often becoming a divided, fragmented person, one
who is totally unaware of an alternative kind of
living, a life imbued with peace, self-acceptance and
wholeness.

Depression, then, can have a positive effect on a
person's life because it rouses a person to life, to
begin the inner journey, to penetrate those dark
aspects from which her mind/soul has fled. To flee
the truth about one's life is to flee from God. Francis
Thompson, a poet of the late nineteenth century, fled

from self-knowledge/God. He sought oblivion in opium, refusing to embark on the inner journey to wholeness. He writes:

I fled Him down the nights and down the days
I fled Him down the arches of the years
I fled Him down the labyrinthine ways
Of my own mind, and in the midst of tears
I hid from him, and under running laughter.
Up vistaed hopes I sped and shot precipitated
Adown titanic glooms of chasmed fears
From those strong feet that followed, followed after
But with unhurrying chase and unperturbed pace,
Deliberate speed, majestic instancy,
They beat, and a Voice beat,
More instant than the feet:
All things betray thee who betrayest me.

Thompson is a Victorian poet, his verse is mandarin style, but he is a modern man who is one of the first poets to refer to the mind, describing it in terms today's reader of poetry would find familiar, 'I fled Him down the labyrinthine ways/Of my own mind.' The metaphor 'labyrinth' for the mind is an ingenious one: it indicates the depth, the breadth, the mystery, the complexity of the mind, one that aptly suggests Jung's paradigm for the mind, one far more complex than Freud's model of superego, ego and id. A labyrinth, is 'a highly complex symbol; it can be a design, a building, an open path, a path enclosed by banks or hedges'. There are two kinds of labyrinths: a unicursal one with a path that leads straight to the centre and out again; and a mulitcursal one, which is a design to puzzle and confuse, with blind paths, requiring a key or solution to the problem.[3] The symbolism of the labyrinth is obvious: the goal is the

centre, which correlates with Jung's theory of individuation, where the goal is the centre, which is the
archetypal Centre, the Self. Thompson is a precursor
of Jung in that he understood that no matter what he
did, how far and fast he fled, he could not escape the
Hound of Heaven, for the 'hound' is his Self, which
has always been with him, echoing Christ's promise,
'And behold, I am with you always, until the end of
time' (Matt. 28:20). Thus, nothing is pursuing
Thompson; he pursues himself through his own
unconscious mind, the abode of the unconscious,
echoing again another of Christ's comments, 'The
kingdom of heaven is within you' (Luke 17:21).
Notice that we often quote the Bible; we do so
because the Bible's language is not always literal but
symbolic. Everyone who has embarked on the inner
journey to wholeness should read the Bible. When
we read the Bible, we are not reading an old, dusty
historical document about the past. We are reading
God's word, the Living God of the past, present and
future, the God of the Living Now Moment who
speaks to us in our now moment wherever we happen to be. We do not have to be in a church or a
chapel or an abbey or a convent for God to speak to
us. He speaks to us through Scripture and through
the 'Scripture' of our souls, within whose depths
abide the universal symbols, the language of the
soul, itself a language that with effort everyone on
earth can learn to understand.

The 'hound' of our soul is the archetypal Self, who,
Jung says, is the Christ. Thus the Self never gives up
on us. It will use every wile, every trick, every ruse,
to lure us to it-Self. If it has to, it will plunge us into
the deep waters of depression, and we will think we
are indeed drowning, but with effort and will we can
surrender to what the unconscious Self encourages

us to learn about ourselves. Yes, we can run, of course, away from the Self, but the Self is the cure that we have long sought and what we need. Thus to flee the Self is to flee from soul-health, from whole-ness. If the soul is ever to achieve peace, it must listen to the Self. Dante learns this profound truth and expresses it in his masterpiece *The Divine Comedy*: 'In his will (Self) is our peace.' And if we do not embrace our journey, we do indeed betray the Self, which simultaneously means that we betray ourselves, for there is no duality, as we are one with the Christ.

We do not exist as inanimate things like a block of wood or a rock. To exist as a human being, we must take hold of our lives, we must delve into the deepest parts of ourselves; we have to ponder our dream life seriously, for dreams are windows into our soul and have much to teach us about ourselves. Thus we must not be passive but proactive about our exist-ence. We do not want to come to the end of our lives and realise that we have not truly lived, what Henry James calls, the 'unlived life'. To live means to face ourselves as well as the world with all the energy and attention we can muster; in fact, it is wise to accept the reality that we are the world, as Jung constantly reminds us because if one person individuates, then that one person does indeed make the world a better place.

How is a person to muster such energy to face depression, to conquer it? As a Christian, a person with depression always has access to prayer. We are enjoined 'to pray continually' (Matt. 26:41). Carl Jung would also encourage his patients to analyse their dreams, to learn how to interpret symbols, for dreams employ a symbolic language; thus, anyone who truly wishes to understand the cause of his or her depression must learn the language of the soul.

Jung would also recommend that we keep a journal near our bed, and when we awaken, immediately record our dreams. If we do not capture our dreams on waking up, we often lose our memory of them; thus, we lose their message because every dream tells us something about us.

Religious rituals can be of tremendous help to people with depression. One of the most enriching religious practices is attendance at Mass. Jung had a profound appreciation of the Mass, implying that the sacrifice of Christ to God in the holy sacrifice of the Mass is similar to what each of us must accomplish in individuation: sometimes to sacrifice our ego to the soul (part of the inner journey into the unconscious) to win wholeness.[4]

A Catholic theologian could not better describe what happens during the Mass. Someone suffering depression is inspired by the Mass to allow all those aspects in herself that lie in darkness to rise. As with the priest who lifts the host and the chalice, the person with depression must raise up from the unconscious those aspects of herself about which she is ashamed, those sins which she has not confessed, those 'negative', dark desires that have a rightful place in her conscious mind. As a participant of the Mass, she asks for God's mercy, but she must also be merciful to herself: she must forgive herself, not just once but always. She must also love herself. In order to become a self-realised, self-actuated person, she has to learn to accept herself as she is. If God accepts her, and he does, how can she dare not accept herself? Not to love and accept herself is to defy God, and it alone can lead to depression.

The great tragedy of the early twentieth century is the First World War. We do not have to analyse its historical causes. We need only know what Carl Jung

has always reminded us: the world is a reflection of
the inner lives of its inhabitants. If people are not at
peace within themselves, it will be manifested in the
external world. Over 5 million men died in the war.
Those who lived to return home were victims of
post-traumatic shock, little understood at the time.
These men were ravaged by the war, seeing and
experiencing horrors they never could previously
have imagined. Many were never to get back on their
feet again, many of them did not have legs; a crip-
pled soldier sitting on a corner selling pencils was a
common sight in London.

The spiritual devastation was also quite visible to
anyone with the eyes to see. Soldiers returned home
to find their former life to be meaningless. Many of
them had lost their faith not only in humanity but
also in God. At this time psychoanalysis began to
thrive as men turned to therapists to help them
adjust to life. Suicides of young men were then a
common event. The novelist Virginia Woolf poign-
antly writes in her novel, *Mrs. Dalloway*, of a former
young soldier who throws himself out of a window
to be impaled on a wrought-iron fence.

Because the Christian belief had been abandoned,
these men had nothing to hold onto, nothing to help
them face and endure their suffering. If they had
turned their gaze upon Christ, had pondered his life,
his passion, his crucifixion, death and resurrection,
they would have found in Christ a model to follow.
The unconscious mind would then have released the
energy and the will for them to pick up their own
cross and carry it. The power of religion helps us to
live, to endure, to find meaning in our suffering;
Christians always have the Christ to behold, and to
behold him is to become him. Christ is what Jung
would call the 'cure of souls'.

These broken men of the war T. S. Eliot later called 'The Hollow Men' (1925). Jung understood their brokenness, but he offered them more than Freud could. Freud dismissed religion as neurosis, but Jung said it was neurosis' cure. He often said that the broken people he worked with as patients were cured when they again accepted a spiritual perspective on life. The soul's natural desire is to be healthy, and if we believe this statement, we can find a cure for anything that ails the modern soul. But first there must be a belief in the soul, for without that belief, we have nothing to hold onto: we cannot hold onto nothingness. Of course, later in the twentieth century, French thinkers will attempt to create a philosophy of nothingness, and for a time it will be the 'new' and chic way of thinking: that life is absurd and means nothing.

Let us, however, return to brokenness. Today there are many people who are broken. Broken by the vicissitudes of life, the loss of loved ones, the loss of self-esteem, the loss of a job, the loss of homes, the loss of belief, the loss of God. And yet, as Jung reminds us, out of our brokenness can come beauty and wholeness, or holiness.

To illustrate our point, let us consider the work of a potter by the name of Rick Dillingham. He is an artist of brinkmanship. He deliberately shatters his bisque-fired pot into pieces, paints each shard, a miniature canvas unto itself, and reconstructs the pot for refirement. The reassembled pottery represents a new, transformed beauty that boldly declares its previous brokenness. In fact, its brokenness renders Dillingham's creations more beautiful and unique, a minimalism turned upside down, illustrating not so much that less is more but that the whole is more than the sum of its parts.

The idea of taking what was broken, what many would consider useless, and of transforming it into something more lovely is life-inspiring. The poet Edward A. Robinson says that most things break, including people. We all break down (for example, with depression) at some point in our lives. It is a fact of life. But great things can emerge from such break-age. We think of the poet Theodore Roethke, a victim of depression all his life, who suffered a nervous breakdown but on recovery said, 'That wasn't a breakdown but a break-up!' because he emerged a saner and more whole person. Ignatius Loyola founded the Society of Jesus after an illness and a spiritual crisis. John of the Cross wrote his greatest poetry while in prison, as the monks of his own order tried to break his spirit. The poet Francis Thompson, broken by addiction to opium, emerged from his dark night to compose his luminous spiritual autobi-ography, 'The Hound of Heaven'. T. S. Eliot emerged from his brokenness, chronicled in *The Waste Land*, to write his spiritual masterpiece, the *Four Quartets*. C. S. Lewis abandoned his atheism and loneliness to write *Surprised by Joy*. Dorothy Day out of her bro-kenness converted to Catholicism and founded the Catholic Worker movement and later wrote her mov-ing story, *The Long Loneliness*.

That we are all broken (fragmented, thus not whole) by sin is knowledge all Christians under-stand. To save us from our brokenness Christ came on earth. He subjected himself to the breaking of the crucifixion only to rise again on the third day. He is the artist par excellence of the broken. He is our example to follow.

Malcolm Muggeridge once said that he never learned much about life or himself when matters went his way; only through suffering did he learn life's most valuable lessons. His 'wasted time' (the name of his autobiography) led him to Christ and to Catholicism.

All those who suffer depression should view their bouts of depression as opportunities to learn about themselves, about their lives, about transforming what is 'broken' about them into something beautiful. To illustrate this point, let us look at the parable of the prodigal son. Here is a broken young man. He once had everything: a family, a loving father, a job, plenty of clothes and food. He was, as we say, 'sitting pretty'. But he demands his inheritance, and ends up squandering it in a life of dissipation until he is a homeless and broken man. When he is feeding the pigs, he realises that his life is shattered (like one of Dillingham's pots). He decides to return home. His elderly father sees him from a distance and runs towards him. No questions asked. Forgiveness is offered unconditionally. His father will listen to no 'mea culpa' and orders his servants to clothe his son in the finest robe, to adorn his hand with a ring, to shod his feet with sandals and to kill the fatted calf for a feast to celebrate the return of his lost son. The father transforms his broken son by the beauty of acceptance and forgiveness symbolised by the new, fine clothes, ring and feast. What is lost is found again, what is broken is whole again.

According to Jung, we have all we need to live beautiful and whole/holy lives within ourselves. We need look nowhere but inside our own souls. We have the potential to transform our brokenness into something quite beautiful, that is, if we do one thing: listen to the still, small voice of the Self. In so doing, we open ourselves to the potentiality of brokenness becoming beautiful and whole.

Let us briefly return to the prodigal son. Where did the impetus come from for him to return to his father? His ego likely coaxed him not to return home because it would be humiliating. He would reveal his failure, his shame, his shattered life. But rising from the unconscious mind was the reminder of his loving father, one who would never reject him, one who would embrace him no matter what he had done with his life. He had a choice: to listen to his ego or listen to the voice of the Self. He chose the latter. We now give Jung the last word: 'Our unconscious energies give momentum to our journey through life and, if we direct their course, our actions will have strength; we may even sense that God is behind us.'[5]

Depression is a message from the unconscious. It reminds us that wholeness of the soul has not been revealed. The person with depression is like a person in an urban high-rise building looking straight out of a window. He does not see much with his staring. What he must do is to go to the window, open it and look below. What will he see? He will see life abundant, people coming and going, cars and trucks, a multitude of colour and a commotion of movement. He will see life going on. With this analogy in mind, someone who is depressed must open the window of his soul, taking a good look into its depths, and there with exquisite attention, he will find life abundant and with it the energy he so much craves to invigorate his mind and soul. Everything we need to live, Jung reminds us, abides within us. All we need do is open the window and LOOK!

Notes

1 *Selected Letters of C. G. Jung, 1909–1961*, ed. Gerhard Adler (Princeton, NJ: Princeton University Press, 1984), p. 140.
2 *C. G. Jung Speaking: Interviews and Encounters*, ed. William McGuire and R. F. C. Hull (Princeton, NJ: Princeton University Press, 1977), p. 449.
3 J. C. Cooper, *An Illustrated Encyclopedia of Traditional Symbols* (London: Thames and Hudson, 1978), p. 92.
4 Carl Jung, *Psyche and Symbol*, ed. Violet S. de Laszlo (New York: Doubleday, 1958), p. 197.
5 *C. G. Jung Speaking*, p. 158.

Questions for reflection

- Can I claim wholeness?
- If I can't, why not and what can I do about it?
- Do I take time for introspection?
- Do I understand my moods and their cause?
- In what ways am I broken?
- Have I tried to transform my brokenness into something whole and beautiful?
- Do I take time to read the New Testament, to learn more about the life and death of Christ?
- Do I try to emulate Christ in my daily life?
- Am I praying every day?
- In my life, am I silent in order to hear the 'still, small voice of God'?
- In my life, am I putting time aside to be alone with the Alone (God)?
- When I am depressed, do I succumb to depression or do I try to rise above it?

- When I am depressed, do I understand that my unconscious is speaking to me?
- Am I making an effort to decipher what the unconscious wants me to know about myself?
- No matter what psychological or spiritual state I find myself in, do I accept myself, or do I find myself blaming and chastising myself?
- Lastly and most importantly, have I forgiven myself for past mistakes?

2
Carl Jung's Theory of Individuation

Individuation is the process by which a person seeks psychological and spiritual wholeness. It is not a passive but an active journey, one that demands we become aware of what is occurring in our conscious and unconscious mind, to live out our own truth, to activate the fullness of our potential, all of which lies within the sovereignty of the soul, as Christ reminds us, 'The kingdom of heaven is within you.'

Individuation's exquisite attention to the inner journey is not narcissism. It is rather an attempt to gain self-knowledge, to understand our longings, our desires, our compulsions, our rage, our fear, our anxiety, our phobias and our guilt. It is also a process requiring us to delve into the causes of our depressions. Most people experience depression (clinical and chemical depression excluded) when the unconscious mind withdraws eros (energy) from the conscious mind to make us focus on our inner lives.

Many people experience depression because they are avoiding aspects of their personality that they wish they did not possess; thus, they repress them into the unconscious mind. However, they do not disappear and eventually make their presence known, and one of the primary ways is to cause a person to become depressed. Therefore, depression is a symptom of a soul in search of health, or what Jung calls wholeness.

In individuation, there are two major archetypes that one must face: for a man, the shadow and the anima; for a woman, the shadow and the animus. Before addressing these two hurdles, let us examine Jung's model of the mind. Jung sees the ego as the centre of the conscious mind; the ego is displayed to the world through or by its persona. Persona is the Latin word for mask. We all have a cast of masks that we wear in life: our student mask, our occupational mask, our social mask, our romantic mask, our familial mask. These masks, Jung says, are a necessary part of life, for they protect us. Without a mask, we display before the world our naked, vulnerable self, and to allow the world to see us this way is to invite a mauling of our selfhood. We remember Christ's dictum, 'Be as shrewd as serpents and simple as doves' (Matt. 10:16). In other words, while living in the world we can retain our vulnerability but we must be shrewd enough not to display it before the world.

There is, however, a danger in wearing masks. We often become too comfortable wearing our masks, one layered over another to the point that we lose contact with our true self. We also over-identify with certain of our masks so that we are again further removed from our authentic self. For instance, the successful lawyer who returns home from court to his wife and children and at dinner pontificates as if he were still in court; he fails to show fatherly interest in his children's life or husbandly interest in his wife's concerns; he insists on his ego being stroked by his 'clients'. The individuated person, however, is keenly aware of his repertoire of masks, knowing when to don them and when to remove them.

Let us now address the first of individuation's great hurdles, coming to terms with the archetypal shadow, the process Jung calls the 'apprentice-piece

of individuation'. As mentioned, the shadow represents aspects of our personality we would rather not
admit to, repressing them into the personal unconscious or projecting them onto other people, so that
we quickly perceive someone we little know as
unkind, cruel, arrogant, selfish, ambitious, envious,
vices or sins that belong not to someone else but to
ourselves, but we do not have the courage to face
ourselves, only aware of the acceptable if not perfect
persona we have constructed for ourselves. Projection of our own 'sins' is echoed in Christ's question,
'Why do you notice the splinter in your brother's
eye, but do not perceive the wooden beam in your
own eye?' (Matt. 7:3).

When depression arrives, therefore, we must take
notice and make an effort to discover its neurotic
cause, for cure lies in knowledge. Often depression is
the result of an 'unlived' aspect of life. For instance, it
may imply that our sexual self is not being lived out
fully. As Christians, we often ignore our physical
longings in favour of our spiritual desires – a dangerous duality. Both body and soul have needs. The
body needs to be pampered; it needs good food,
exercise; it needs access to air, sky, sea and land. It
needs to touch and be touched, reminding us of the
poet Anne Sexton's verse, 'Touch is all.'

There are so many touch-starved people in the
world, people raised in puritanical homes where
bodily needs were ignored, punished or disparaged.
Thus, they assumed as a way of life an unnatural
asceticism, one so deeply rooted in the personality
that it saps all joy from life. There is nothing sinful
about the erotic. A person who discovers and nur-
tures sexuality is a person who has discovered a
wonderful domain of joy. With a healthy attitude, not
one of disdain or guilt, a person becomes the master

of his domain, not a slave to it. A promiscuous person is one who has lost control of sexuality, becoming a victim to its every whim. A whole person understands that sexuality is not the continent of one's personality, only a part of it; therefore, a healthy perspective is maintained.

How do we win such control and balance? Consider the deep-sea diver, one exploring a place where a Spanish ship with treasures has sunk. The diver must be willing to dive into a deep and dangerous part of the sea; she is willing to take the risk because she knows this particular sunken ship has trunks of gold and jewels. The ego is like a diver, plunging into the deep waters of the psyche, into the unconscious. She will find items encrusted by the sands of time, but if brought to the surface of the conscious mind, she can examine them, 'clean' them with attention and discover that what appeared to be dark, ugly matters are really sparkling gems. Every piece of self-knowledge we bring up from the deep sea of our unconscious will glow with light, enlightening our conscious mind with self-knowledge. But the process is as dangerous as that of the deep-sea diver: we may run out of air, become lost, encounter unexpected dangers; we may be overwhelmed by the power of the sea, but everything worth pursuing in life demands risk, and everyone, according to Jung, is called upon to be the hero of his or her life journey. Not to take the risk is to live an 'unlived' life, which is akin to death-in-life. The latter refers to people who really are not living; they merely exist, like a rock or a lopped-off trunk of a tree.

What keeps many people from embarking upon the inner journey of individuation is doubt. Self-doubt can prevent our becoming whole persons, and Jung was very much aware of this fear. He writes:

Our needs and desires are always active. Trouble occurs only if they are active in the unconscious, if we do not take them consciously in hand so as to give them a definite form and direction. If we refuse to do this, we are dragged along by them and become their victim. Then they are like a sledge rushing downhill in the snow, with no one at the steering ropes. You must place yourself firmly at the steering ropes, not hang on at the back or, worse, be unwilling to take the ride at all; that only lands you in panic. Our unconscious energies give momentum to our journey through life and, if we direct their course, our actions will have strength; we may even sense that God is behind us.[1]

Jung describes the integration of the anima and animus archetypes as the 'masterpiece of individuation'. He theorised that people are psychologically androgynous. A man has an inner woman, the anima; a woman has an inner man, the animus. To be in a healthy relationship with one's counter-sexual self requires much soul work.

For a man to understand whether or not he is on firm ground with his anima, he must examine his relationships with women in the real world. He must be attentive to how he treats women. If he finds that he is unkind, cutting, satirical, insensitive, disrespectful, critical or indifferent towards women, then he indeed has a problem. It is a problem because he is projecting his true feelings for a woman; if they are all negative and misogynistic, then he has much inner work to accomplish.

Another way for him to understand his relationship with the feminine archetype is to analyse his dreams. The anima will communicate with a man in dreams. If she feels neglected or poorly treated, she will make it known. Our culture abounds with anima archetypes represented by a number of figures. In Renaissance Europe, painters' favourite subject was the Madonna and Child. Such masterpieces by Michelangelo, Botticelli, Raphael, da Vinci, all point to an acceptance of the importance of the feminine in everyday life. But the anima archetype is Janus-faced: it has two sides, one loving, one destructive. We think of figures like Medea and Lady Macbeth. We think of the mythology surrounding the belief in witches, primarily negative projections of men. In contrast to the negative, we also think of the Muses, the source of men's creativity.

In modern literature, we think of Nabokov's Lolita, the story of a middle-aged man who has lost his life force until Humbert Humbert meets the young, energetic 12-year-old Lolita, who infuses Humbert with new life. One can read Nabokov's as a story of a pervert, a paedophile, or one can read it as a story of a man who has lost contact with all that is fine and good about the anima. It is not uncommon for middle-aged, repressed men to fall in love with young women. It is indicative that a man has lost touch with his inner woman. We will later see how this particular loss affected the Trappist monk Thomas Merton.

A man too often lives his life from an intellectual perspective, ignoring all feeling, all emotions, a spiritual imbalance that will eventually take a toll on a man. He will tend to grow into a cold, unfeeling, insensitive man unable to take joy in his wife, his children and his friends. Anima is the archetype that offers a man energy to reach out to the world, to embrace it. Without eros a man will close himself off from life. He will reduce his social circle; he will prefer to stay home and avoid social occasions. He will find escape from life in his work or in books or in hobbies. In general, he becomes a victim of the 'unlived' life, the very danger Henry James warns us about in his novel *The Ambassadors*. Through his character Strether, James says:

> Live all you can; it's a mistake not to. It doesn't so much matter what you do in particular, so long as you have your life. If you haven't had that, what have you had? Do what you like so long as you don't make my mistake. For it was a mistake. Live!

To live fully, a man needs to be in a healthy relationship with his anima. If he maintains a positive partnership with his anima (a woman with her animus), then he will likely project that positive image on the woman with whom he will fall in love. At first, a man indeed falls in love with an image, a projection. In time, he will be able to see the woman he married as she truly is, stripped of his projections. She will in all likelihood remain the loved woman, but it will be a more real love because a man now sees unclouded by his projections. What is to be kept in mind is that in the beginning of love, the future wife already possessed the 'hook' of her beloved's inner woman; thus, when he does finally 'know' his wife (think of Mary's saying to the angel 'I have not known man'), she steps quite comfortably and beautifully into his dream image.

    Many of those who suffer from depression are people who have not experienced the inner marriage of opposites, of a man with his anima, of a woman with her animus. When a man does indeed integrate his anima, he is reborn and transformed. Depression is lifted, and a man is flooded with new energy. He wants to live again, not pine away in a darkened, lonely room. He wants again to connect with life, which means he reaches out to people again, establishes or renews friendships. If he is married, his marriage takes on a new life, enlivening not only himself but his spouse. He also begins to consider his spiritual life, his relationship with God. He returns to God, to his church, to Mass and to prayer because not only is he again reconnected with what is seen but with what is unseen ('We see through a glass darkly', 1 Cor. 13:12).

Let us look at a depressed man. A good example is Shakespeare's 'Sonnet 29':

When in disgrace with Fortune and men's eyes,
I all alone beweep my outcast state,
And trouble deaf heaven with my bootless cries,
And look upon myself and curse my fate,
Wishing me like to one more rich in hope,
Featured like him, like him with friends possessed,
Desiring this man's art, and that man's scope,
With what I most enjoy contented least;
Yet in these thoughts myself almost despising,
Haply I think on thee, and then my state
(Like to the lark at break of day arising
From sullen earth) sings hymns at heaven's gate,
For thy sweet love rememb'red such wealth brings
That then I scorn to change my state with kings.

Our speaker is in disgrace not only with Fortune and her wheel, but he is in disgrace with humankind. He is so depressed by his alienation, his loneliness ('all alone') that he can but 'beweep' his state of soul and mind. As with many depressed people, he prays for relief to God, but heaven seems to be deaf to his 'bootless cries', cries that go nowhere. Self-pity often attacks people with depression, and here too the speaker looks upon himself and curses his fate. He then exacerbates his negative mind-set by comparing himself to others, always a dangerous mental game. He sees all around him better-looking men, men with more friends, men who have greater talent ('art') and greater knowledge ('scope'). Even what he most enjoys cannot offer him contentment. He is now at the point of 'almost despising' himself. The key word is 'almost'. Why does he not despise himself? Because he happens to remember that there is someone out there, a woman, who loves him. She is the anima figure who saves him. Her power of love is so great that this greatly depressed man is by her memory reinvigorated, and his depression dissipates so that his spirit (soul) rises, like the 'lark at break of day arising from sullen earth'. The bird's song correlates with the speaker's song, this very sonnet, a hymn of beauty about his beloved. The thought of her renders him so happy that he would not change his place with that of kings. Why? Because his anima (his queen) has already bestowed kingship upon him. The speaker journeys from the throes of depression and despair to 'heaven's gate'. Such is the power of the anima. Such is the power of love.

We will now look at an individuated literary figure, Shakespeare's Prospero from *The Tempest*. His name alone alerts us, for when we read his name, we naturally think of the word 'prosperous'. The dictionary definition is flourishing, well-to-do and well-off. Prospero (also derived from the Latin for hope) is not well-off in a materialistic way; he is rich with knowledge, the kind of knowledge that has led him to psychological and spiritual wholeness (wellness).

His brother usurped his Milan throne and cast both his daughter Miranda and him to sea with little chance of their surviving. Prospero is partly responsible for losing his kingdom, for he paid too much attention to his books and not enough attention to his duties as a ruler. His daughter and he found safety on an island where Prospero is monarch of all he surveys. His servants are the spirit Ariel and the half-man Caliban (the word derived from cannibal). Because of a storm magically conjured by Prospero, all of Prospero's enemies, including his brother Antonio, have arrived at his island (by Prospero's magic, none are wet). He has some fun making them fearful and uncomfortable, but his true purpose is to forgive all who have harmed him.

He has not wasted his time on the island. He has not spent it plotting revenge on Antonio who stole his throne from him. He has books, and he has devoted time to the study of ancient wisdom and of magic. He is now a mage, a magician. He commands nature and all the spirits of the island. The kind of magic he has cultivated is a holy one.

The art by which Prospero controls nature is the disciplined use of holy knowledge, or white magic: as such it is distinct from the black magic of the witch Sycorax, who by union with the devil can exploit nature for evil purposes. Prospero's instrument is reason, which he exercises through the grace of God and through which he can liberate the spirit of nature – symbolised by Ariel – and control both the brute forces of nature and his own passions. His art is that of civilisation, imbued with divine purpose and capable of controlling the external world by the exercise of virtue. Representing as he does the power of mind as opposed to that of the senses, he stands for chastity, just as Caliban stands for sexual promiscuity. Chastity is the quality of Christ, the essential symbol of civilisation by which a man controls his own animalism. The severity with which he applies its control to the young love of Ferdinand and Miranda is thus to be expected.[2]

Ariel and Caliban symbolise two aspects of his personality, Ariel his soul, and Caliban his body. When he frees Ariel at the end of the play, he frees himself to explore for the rest of his life his inner soulscape. The monster-like Caliban symbolises Prospero's shadow, his dark, instinctual (sexual) desires. He, however, is not frightened by his dark side. He says of Caliban, 'This thing of darkness I acknowledge mine.'

An individuated person is one who experiences an inner marriage of opposites. For Prospero, the spirit (Ariel) and the body (Caliban) are united and claimed, a psychic event Jung names *coniunctio*. The latter is a word often used in the study of alchemy, a study Jung took seriously. At first it referred to chemical combinations, but Jung uses it in psychological terms to describe any marriage of opposites.

So, in Prospero, what do we have? We have a wise man able to forgive old enemies. Thus, his ego is not inflated; therefore, he can look upon another and see the person free of his (Prospero's) own projections. Only a person who has come to terms with his own sins, has forgiven and accepted himself, can forgive another.

As a father figure, Prospero greatly loves his daughter Miranda; he is pleased by the prospect of Miranda's marriage to Alonso's (King of Naples) son Ferdinand. He understands the holy nature of marriage; he wants his daughter and future son-in-law to be happy in the *coniunctio* of sacramental marriage. He wisely understands the beauty of marriage because he has won wisdom from his acceptance of his dual nature, that of soul and body, an acceptance allowing an inner marriage whose fruit is psychic and spiritual wholeness, whereas the fruit of Miranda and Ferdinand will be new life. Prospero is indeed an individuated person. He has accomplished his soul-work, and he can now return to the world. His last words (Epilogue) are revelatory:

> Now I want
> Spirits to enforce, art to enchant;
> And my ending is despair
> Unless I be reliev'd by prayer,
> Which pierces so that it assaults
> Mercy itself and frees all faults.
> As you from crimes would pardon'd be,
> Let your indulgence set me free.

Such generosity of spirit! Prospero turns to prayer in order to assault Mercy (God) itself. He holds no grudges, no blame, no ill-feelings; he embraces forgiveness for everyone. He embraces unconditional love, agape.

If asked to describe a person who had never embarked on individuation, I would turn to Shakespeare's King Lear.

When we first meet Lear, he is still very much the King, a powerful ruler before whom everyone bows in homage and in fear. His every wish is his command, quickly carried out, his every desire fulfilled, his every request completed. He is a man whose life has been lived from his ego. His gaze has never turned inward towards his soul, nor has it ever been unselfishly fixed upon another human being. He is a monster of egotism.

He calls for a meeting to announce that he is ready to step down as king and deliver his kingdom over to his three daughters, Goneril, Regan and Cordelia. His intention is actually an abrogation of his responsibility, indicative of a man who has rarely been very much aware of anything but himself, his own comfort and satisfaction.

He demands of his daughters, 'Which of you shall we say doth love us most?' (1:1:54). Lear's true intent is to have his ego stroked by playing a game whose end, unbeknown to anyone, is already fixed. He will apportion his kingdom according to how much each daughter loves him, but he has already decided to offer the richest and largest part of his kingdom to his favourite daughter, Cordelia.

Goneril and Regan try to outdo each other in praising their father, flattering him with a love, they say, that knows no bounds, a love dearer than their own eyesight, indeed, dearer to them than their own lives. Lear is mightily pleased and offers them goodly portions of his kingdom. When it is Cordelia's turn to speak, she says nothing, which at first perplexes Lear, but it then angers him, and he warns her, 'Nothing will come of nothing' (1:1:99). She still refuses to flatter him, saying that unlike her sisters she cannot offer him all her love, preserving some for her future husband. Her comment enrages Lear who swiftly disowns his daughter, banishing her to France with her husband, the King of France.

After Lear has given all away, against the advice of his chief advisor whom he has also rashly banished, his two daughters begin their campaign to strip Lear of his knights, his power, his prestige, his servants, and his crown, which he still insists on wearing. When former servants do not jump at his command, when his daughters fail to meet with him, he finally realises how foolish he was to give away his kingdom. He is now a powerless man.

From a Jungian perspective Lear's inflated ego has been deflated. His kingly mask has been stripped away. He has been stripped of a king's trappings: his knights, his power, influence, money and privileges. He is in effect a nobody. He himself has rejected the one person who loves him: Cordelia. Her name derives from the Latin *cors, cordis*, meaning love. He has rejected love, and in Jungian terms, he has rejected his anima. He is a man at the last crossroad of life, and because he is old, it is likely his last opportunity to achieve wisdom, thus wholeness.

The stripping process is important. Jungian Father Josef Goldbrunner writes:

> To live a spiritually healthy life one must find one's own truth and to find one's own truth the natural soul must be laid bare; one must consciously come to terms with the irrational forces within oneself, incorporating them into the total life of the soul, but never allowing them a perfectly free rein ... stripping the soul is an essential part of the hygiene and culture of the soul. It makes the personality deeper, clearer, and more embracing. Laying the soul bare is a form of loyalty to one's own ground-plan ... When the soul does not live its own truth, the vision of God's truth also becomes clouded, for spiritual disease involves our whole thinking, our feeling and willing and even what our senses perceive.[3]

Lacking self-knowledge, Lear laments to his fool, 'Who is it that can tell me who I am?' (1:4:236), an echo of his daughter Regan's remark that Lear 'hath ever but slenderly known himself' (1:1:340). Because he has renounced his kingly power, Lear has unconsciously propelled himself upon a journey, the journey of individuation, one that will be a difficult and painful one for him. However, it is a necessary journey, otherwise he would die as a man never knowing himself, never knowing what it means to be true to himself, never attaining psychic and spiritual wholeness. Thus, King Lear's life would indeed fall under the description of tragic, but by the conclusion of the play Lear, we will see, redeems himself.

Lear finds himself in a terrible tempest out on the heath. The thunder and lightning remind him of the tempest within his own mind: he is not yet aware of it, but he is undergoing a great 'sea change', a transformation of personality that will require a loss of sanity, a descent into the unconscious, a state Shakespeare describes as madness; but he will, however, emerge a changed man, a man granted a second chance, a man offered the opportunity to be authentic.

The first sign of his transformation occurs when Lear and the fool are about to flee the tempest by entering a nearby hovel. Lear says to the fool, 'In, boy, go first – You houseless poverty, Nay, get thee in', a remarkable moment in the play. For the first time in his life, Lear has thought of someone else first, allowing the fool to enter the hovel before the king; it is a poignant moment of kindness, of unselfishness. His next comment is also important, 'I'll pray, and then I'll sleep.' *King Lear* is a pre-Christian play, but Shakespeare himself was Christian. In tempestuous times, either of nature or of our souls and minds, Christians have always recognised the necessity of prayer.

Lear returns alone to the heath, with rain pouring down on him. The rain is akin to baptismal waters, for Lear is reborn, and his soliloquy is not merely a monologue, it is in fact a prayer:

Poor naked wretches, wheresoe'er you are,
That bide the pelting of this pitiless storm,
How shall your houseless heads and unfed sides,
Your looped and windowed raggedness defend you
From seasons such as these? O, I have ta'en
Too little care of this. Take physic, pomp.
Expose thyself to feel what wretches feel,
That thou may'st shake the superflux to them
And show the heavens more just.

Notice that he is not thinking of himself but of 'poor naked wretches', wherever they are in the world, definitely an echo of Christ's command that we should, as his followers, clothe the naked and feed the hungry and house the homeless. Lear thinks of the poor with their 'looped and windowed' clothes, clothes so ragged they would not keep their wearer dry or warm. And then the utterly honest admission that Lear, once a king of a land populated with his subjects, has 'ta'en too little care of this'. He has failed as a king because he did not care about the poor of his kingdom, the hungry, the naked, the homeless. He realises now that he must expose himself to suffering in order to understand it: 'Expose thyself to feel what wretches feel.' It is a supreme moment in the transformation of a monster of egotism.

To whom are Lear's words directed? It appears that Lear is addressing all those in the world who, like himself, are suffering in this pelting storm. These are words, however, that rise not from the conscious but the unconscious that has caused his own tempest in the mind. Shakespeare often juxtaposes matters in nature to correlate with events in his characters' lives. A frightening storm upon the heath matches the even more frightening storm in Lear's mind, for he is about to enter into the kingdom of madness, the descent into the purging fires of the dark night of the soul.

In Christian terms, Lear has made his confession. He has 'owned' his sins. He no longer, as he previously said, is a man 'more sinned against than sinning'. He knows the absurdity of such a comment. He has sinned, and he has confessed his sins, and now the next step is redemption. His penance, however, is a demanding one: his mind will leave the world for a time. He will no longer be of this world. He dies to himself, only later to be resurrected. All of which confirms the Christian paradigm, one that Jung highly respected.

We know that when Christ died, he visited hell. In his madness, where has Lear gone? Perhaps madness is Lear's purgatory. His being is trying to connect with the archetypal centre of the psyche: the Self. Lear's life has for far too long been centred upon his ego. It is now time for him to centre his life upon the Self. It requires a lonely, unaccompanied inner journey, one that will demand that he face the monsters of his own ego: his failures as a man, a husband, a father, a friend, and as a king. Because his ego is so strong, it will fight recognition of failure. Thus, the unconscious employs its most frightening and powerful tool to lead Lear into the light of self-knowledge: its antithesis, madness.

It is a sad sight to see Lear after madness descends upon him. There is another stripping process: he removes his clothes to become one of the 'naked wretches' he spoke about, and he clothes himself with leaves and flowers. When he meets the blinded Gloucester, for he momentarily returns to himself and recognises poor Gloucester and is moved to compassion by his friend's loss of eyes, he says:

If thou wilt weep my fortunes, take my eyes.
I know thee well enough; thy name is Gloucester.
Thou must be patient.

Notice that Lear has long abandoned the royal plural, and now simply refers to himself by the simple singular pronoun 'I'. Notice also his generous gift of his eyes, eyes blind to his own personae, eyes blind to love when it stood before him in the form of Cordelia, eyes blind to the suffering of his people, blind to the loyalty of his friend Kent. Notice also the sum total of his wisdom: 'Thou must be patient.' Has not patience been long advocated as one of the greatest Christian virtues, one Carl Jung understood profoundly? He always warned his patients that the inner journey to wholeness is one that is not accomplished in a day or a week, it may take a lifetime; therefore, it requires patience. In matters psychological and spiritual, not to be considered a duality, patience is the ultimate wisdom: Love is patient, love is kind (1 Cor. 13:4).

We now come to love: Cordelia. When Cordelia hears about the way her father has been mistreated, she sets out for Britain with an army. Her men find Lear and dress him in 'fresh garments'. Clothes here symbolised the New Man who is soon to emerge from his deep sleep. When Lear opens his old eyes, he sees Cordelia. He is still confused, but his confusion begins to clear:

I am a very foolish fond old man,
Fourscore and upward, not an hour more nor less,
And to deal plainly,
I fear I am not in my perfect mind.
Methinks I should know you and know this man,
Yet I am doubtful, for I am mainly ignorant
What place this is, and all the skill I have
Remembers not these garments; nor I know not
Where I did lodge last night. Do not laugh at me,
For, as I am a man, I think this lady
To be my child Cordelia.

These words are a great distance from Lear's first words to his children, 'Which of you shall we say doth love us most?' Notice again the dropping of the royal plural: Cordelia is not 'our' child but 'my child'. Notice also his description of himself as old, foolish and fond (silly, dazed). Lear now knows himself, and he recognises his daughter. He then asks for forgiveness: 'Pray you now, forget and forgive. I am old and foolish.' And Cordelia weeps for her father.

In the end we must always face the choice of loving and forgiving or not loving and forgiving, not only ourselves but others.

Cordelia's forces are defeated by Edmund, and she and Lear are taken as prisoners. Lear tries to console his daughter:

Come, let's away to prison.
We two alone will sing like birds i' th' cage.

When thou dost ask me a blessing, I'll kneel down
And ask of thee forgiveness.

Thus the play ends upon Lear's eloquent use of
language that can only be described as Christian:
blessing, kneeling and forgiveness. For Lear, the
ideal life now is somewhat similar to a monk in his
cell where he can kneel, pray and ask forgiveness.
His very last words, however, are harrowing. At
Edmund's order Cordelia and Lear are both to be
killed. Lear survives but not his daughter, and in the
last scene, we see him carrying her in his arms, a
reverse Pièta, the father carrying the sacrifice of his
daughter. His final words are, 'Never, never, never,
never, never.' Cordelia will never again live on this
earth, and it breaks Lear's heart. When he dies, his
eyes are fixed upon the face of the daughter who
unconditionally loved him.

Most people describe *King Lear* as a tragedy. However, although imbued with much suffering, *King
Lear* is a story of triumph. Lear has finally won
wholeness; he finally recognises and embraces love;
he learns humility and forgiveness. And in the very
last moment of his life, he gazes upon love: Cordelia.

Let us give the last word on Lear to Jungian psy-
chologist Maud Bodkin:

> Lear (in the last scene) has been lifted up, a
> portent to mankind but one sacred and fraught
> with comfort – a vision of man's essential
> nature and destiny, beheld under the form of
> eternity, from which taint of mortal sin and
> delusion is purged away.
>
> The tragic hero, seen under this aspect as a
> sacrificial, profoundly representative, has a
> clear relation to the Christ of the Gospel story.

In Christ appears pre-eminently this character felt obscurely in such heroes of poetic tragedy as Oedipus and Lear. Christ is the sacred object lifted up, fraught with comfort for man, gazing upon whom he sees, as in a transfiguring mirror, his own soul purified and delivered.[4]

Notes

1 *C. G. Jung Speaking: Interviews and Encounters*, ed. Willian McGuire and R. F. C. Hull (Princeton, NJ: Princeton University Press, 1977), p. 158.
2 William Shakespeare, *The Tempest*, ed. George Lyman Kittredge (Lexington: Xerox College Publishing, 1967), p. xv.
3 Joseph Goldbrunner, *Wholeness is Holiness* (New York: Pantheon Books, 1954), pp. 31–2.
4 Maud Bodkin, *Archetypal Patterns in Poetry: Psychological Studies of Imagination* (London: Oxford University Press, 1934), pp. 280–4.

Questions for reflection

- Have I yet embarked upon the inner journey?
- Am I an egotistical person? If so, what actions can I take to become 'other' conscious?
- Do I find myself projecting my own negative qualities upon others?
- As a man, do I find myself often critical of women?
- As a woman, do I find myself often critical of men?

- Am I aware of wearing personae (masks)?
- Am I aware that a persona does not represent my true Self?
- Am I hard on myself, finding it difficult to forgive my failures?
- Am I devoting enough time to prayer?
- Do I pray for wholeness/holiness?

3

The Anima and the Shadow

THE ANIMA

We know that Jung's theory of individuation includes his concept of the archetypal anima or animus. Every man possesses an inner woman, the anima. Every woman possesses an inner man, the animus. Each must integrate his or her archetype in order to achieve psychological wholeness. If either a man or a woman is at odds with his or her respective archetype, he or she will experience psychic turbulence both on the unconscious and conscious level.

When a man is positively in touch with his anima, he is kind, open, generous, gentle, assured of his masculinity. If he is a father, he is a sensitive parent, unafraid to express his love and affection to children of both sexes. He has a loving relationship with his wife because he not only loves her but also respects her unique individuality. Responsibility for raising the children and the running of a home are shared by him and his wife.

If he is an administrator at work, he is a fair and just boss. He treats the women who work for him with dignity; he is not threatened by women, who are perhaps gifted in the very field in which himself may excel. He would never interfere in the advancement of a woman, and he would be fair and just in his evaluations of them. He can be this type of man because he is in touch with his anima, having successfully integrated it into his conscious mind.

However, if a man has experienced a negative relationship with a woman, it may interfere with his individuation because it will likely cause him to project his negativity upon the women with whom he lives and works and socialises. It might take years for him to address his misogyny because he has so deeply repressed it that he remains unaware of it. Much of a man's perspective of the feminine is based on his first experiences with his mother. If the relationship between mother and son was not a nurturing one, the male may indeed have difficulty with women in the future.

For example, let us examine the character Hamlet. Hamlet has returned to Denmark for the funeral rites of his father. His mother has hastily married her husband's brother Claudius, a marriage that has infuriated Hamlet who views the marriage as immoral. The law forbade such a marriage between family members; a brother-in-law was considered too close. Thus, according to the culture of the play, the marriage is incestuous. Hamlet is not only angry about it, but he is also ashamed. To him his mother is now a fallen woman.

His rage builds up, even more so when his mother is kind to him and pleads with him not to return so soon to university. All his emotions cry for release. Upon whom does Hamlet spew his rage? He rains it down on his girlfriend Ophelia, the sweet, naive, daughter of Polonius, King Claudius's advisor. Meeting Ophelia, Hamlet verbally attacks her:

> Get thee to a nunnery. Why wouldst thou be a breeder of sinners … I have heard of your paintings too, well enough. God hath given you one face, and you make yourselves another. You jig and amble, and you lisp; you

> nickname God's creatures and make your
> wantonness your ignorance. Go to, I'll no more
> on 't. It hath made me mad. I say we will have
> no more marriage. Those that are married al-
> ready, all but one shall live. The rest shall keep
> as they are. To a nunnery go. (3:1)

These are ugly, shameful words to direct to a young,
innocent girl. It is obvious, however, that Hamlet
sees before him not Ophelia but his mother, but it is
upon Ophelia that he projects his hateful, negative
feelings for his mother. Not only does he project
them onto an individual, but upon all women. Therefore, to him all women are whores, who breed sin-
ners. They paint their faces, gig and dance to attract
men to sin. And as for marriage, he will tolerate those
already married but there is one that shall not live:
his mother's. He then orders Ophelia to a 'nunnery'.
Most people assume he means a convent, but a nunnery was often used mockingly to mean a brothel. He
is, therefore, telling Ophelia to get herself to a
brothel, having reduced all women to prostitutes.

His words are like daggers to Ophelia. She is
shocked and grievously wounded by them. This is
not the Hamlet with whom she fell in love. Not the
Hamlet who was kind to her, offered her love gifts.
Not the Hamlet who was always gentle in word and
deed. Not the Hamlet who was always a gentleman.
In fact, she does not know the man before her, and
she is psychologically shaken by the encounter. She
will never be the same person. She has lost her innocence; not her virginity, but her innocent view of the
world and of men. In the end she will take her life.
Take away her love, and one takes away her reason
for living. Our heart goes out to her. But at the same
time, we feel great pity for Hamlet, for on a deep

level he feels that he has been betrayed by the feminine, the anima archetype. He had always loved his mother, but her marriage is a betrayal not only of his father but of the moral code of the time. Her marriage is incest; he cannot face it or absorb it. As he says, it has made him 'mad'. He has become an unbalanced young man; today, we would immediately place him in therapy.

He is not finished, however, with expressing his anger. His obliquely expressed anger towards Ophelia will prove not to be a sufficient release. He must say what he feels and thinks directly to his mother. Having been summoned by his mother, he says he intends to play the mirror, and reflect back to her, her soul. Gertrude is frightened, for she has never seen him like this, angry and nearly out of control. He says:

> And let me wring your heart; for I shall
> If it be made of penetrable stuff,
> If damned custom have not brazed it so
> That it be proof and bulwark against sense.

Queen Gertrude says, 'What have I done that thou dar'st wag thy tongue, in noise so rude against me?' He replies:

> Such an act
> That blurs the grace and blush of modesty,
> Calls virtue hypocrite, takes off the rose
> From the fair forehead of an innocent love
> And sets a blister there, makes marriage vows
> As false as dicers' oaths – O, such a deep
> As from the body of contraction plucks
> The very soul, and sweet religion makes
> A rhapsody of words! Heaven's face does glow

O'er this solidity and compound mass
With the heated visage, as against the doom,
Is thought-sick at the act. (3:4)

Keep in mind that Hamlet's mother is the Queen of
Denmark. He is her son and subject. To speak to her
in this manner is beyond rude; uttered by anyone
else he could be put to death for it. She, his mother,
loves him, and she wants to know why he speaks to
her so rudely. He speaks in generalities, for he cannot
speak specificically. Her act is one that blurs mod-
esty, takes the rose from the forehead and in its place
substitutes the blister of sexual disease, pledges marriage vows to break them, and acts in such a way that
heaven itself blushes with shame.

Gertrude is amazed. Her marriage was indeed
approved by the court of Denmark, even though it
was stretching the law. She, of course, has no idea
that Hamlet has communed with the ghost of King
Hamlet; she has no knowledge that her new husband
murdered his brother to gain the throne. Gertrude is
innocent of her husband's regicide and fratricide,
and it shows in her utter surprise and shock.

What we want to remember is that Hamlet's
former image of the feminine, a positive one, has
been shattered by his mother's 'o'er hasty marriage',
and by the revelations of the Ghost. Yet the Ghost has
not spoken any negative word against Gertrude,
only against Claudius, and the ghost has ordered his
son to seek revenge only against Claudius and not
Gertrude. Such damage has been done, however, to
Hamlet's image of the feminine, it might not be possible for him ever again to trust any woman.

What would a Jungian therapist say to him? He
would warn him not to generalise about women. He
would encourage him to control his emotions, to see

that he is involved in an act of psychological projection, and that it is indeed possible to take back his projections. For instance, a therapist would counsel Hamlet to stop and think, and to really look at Ophelia, and would ask him, 'What do you see?' Hamlet then, if he is truly not mad, should be able to see the lovely young woman before him, she who has nothing to do with Gertrude and what Gertrude has done with her life.

Let us allow Jungian Jolande Jacobi to have the final word on the anima or animus:

> The encounter with anima and animus makes it possible for us to apprise ourselves of our contra-sexual traits in all their manifestations and to accept at least a part of the qualities projected on the male or female partner as belonging to our own selves, though as a rule this is not accomplished without violent resistances. What man will recognize or accept his moodiness, his unreliability, his sentimentality, and all the other allegedly 'feminine' vices, as his own characteristics instead of chalking them up to the nearest female in his vicinity? And what woman will be persuaded to admit that her immovable opinions and arguments are begotten by bogus logic which stems from her own unconscious masculinity. Once they are made conscious and are no longer projected, but are experienced as belonging to oneself, as realities and agencies within the psyche, anima and animus become symbols of its power to procreate and to give birth: everything new and creative owes its existence to them. They are the fount from which all artistic productivity flows.[1]

THE SHADOW

The shadow archetype represents those aspects of our personality we would rather not recognise or accept. We repress the shadow into the unconscious. But too often we release our shadow onto other people by our projections. When we judge someone to be envious or arrogant or cruel, we are often projecting qualities that in truth we own, but rather than see them in ourselves, we choose to see them in others (unconsciously). Jung is emphatic in his belief that the more of the shadow we bring into the light of consciousness, the more whole we become as human beings. Jungian Jolande Jacobi writes:

> People who believe their ego represents the whole of their psyche, and who neither know nor want to know all the other qualities that belong to it, are wont to project their unknown 'soul parts' into the surrounding world for everything unconscious is first experienced in projection, as qualities of objects. These are those well-known people who always think they are in the right, who in their own eyes are quite blameless and wonderful, but always find everybody else difficult, malicious, hateful, and the source of all their troubles. Nobody likes to admit his own darkness, for which reason most people put up – even in analytical work – the greatest resistance to the realization of their shadow.[2]

To illustrate Jung's concept of the shadow, let us again turn to Shakespeare, who more than any other writer in the English language has captured the power and significance of universal archetypes. We turn to his play *Macbeth*.

In the beginning of Macbeth, King Duncan is so pleased by Macbeth's valour and loyalty to him that he bestows upon him the title of Thane of Cawdor. Macbeth is shocked to hear of his new title because he had met three witches who hailed him with three different titles: first as of Thane of Glamis, a title he owned, then as Thane of Cawdor, a title of a living man, and then as 'king thereafter'. When he hears himself greeted as Thane of Cawdor, he begins to wonder if kingship is also within his grasp. He had thought of being king before, a secret ambition he had shared with his wife Lady Macbeth. As much as he wants to be king, however, he decides to do nothing, saying, 'If chance will have me king, chance may crown me, without my stir.' In other words, why do anything, when chance may drop the crown onto his head as it has with the title Thane of Cawdor (the second of the witches' prophesies that proved to be true)?

Macbeth has written to his wife informing her of the witches' prophesies, and that he is now Thane of Cawdor. She is nearly ecstatic for her husband, as ambitious to be queen as he is to be king. Her reaction to her husband's letter is frightening because she is more determined than Macbeth is to see the crown upon her husband's head, and she is not about to trust in chance. She will take matters into her own hands. She calls upon the powers of darkness (the very powers to which the witches are linked) to 'unsex me here, and fill me from crown to the toe top-full of direst cruelty'. In other words, remove my feminine sexuality, all that is tender, soft, loving, nurturing, motherly, and make me into the cruellest of men:

Make thick my blood
Stop th' access and passage of remorse,

That no compunctious visitings of nature
Shake my fell purpose, nor keep peace between
Th' effect and it. Come to my woman's breasts
And take my milk for gall, you murd'ring ministers
Wherever in your sightless substances
You wait on nature's mischief. Come, thick night,
And pall thee in the dunnest smoke of hell,
That my keen knife see not the wound it makes,
Nor heaven peep through the blanket of the dark
To cry 'Hold, hold.'

The above is one of the most terrifying speeches ever made by a female character outside Greek tragedy (for example, Medea and Clytemnestra). Lady Macbeth renounces all her femininity in order to become a monster that stops at nothing to win what she desires. She dismisses her husband as being 'too full o' the milk of human kindness to catch the nearest way' to the throne. Her husband is basically a good and gentle man off the battleground. But she will have the milk of her own breasts replaced by gall to achieve her end, and her weapon of choice is the phallic 'keen knife'.

Little does Macbeth know that his wife will be the one to push him into regicide. We cannot blame her completely, for both share equal responsibility for what they do. And to be fair and honest, the first to present the idea of regicide was indeed Macbeth, whose mind, repulsed by the idea, represses it into the unconscious mind.

King Duncan has decided to honour Macbeth with a visit to his castle. Lady Macbeth immediately concocts a plan to murder the saintly king. Macbeth himself has decided that there is no good reason to murder Duncan except, 'vaulting ambition', and refuses to give in to his desires. Lady Macbeth, how-

ever, is appalled that her husband has so quickly
given up what he most desires. And she knows her
husband well, and knows how to attack him:

Was hope drunk
Wherein you dressed yourself? Hath it slept since?
And wakes it now, to look so green and pale
At what it did so freely? From this time
Such I account thy love. Art thou afeard
To be the same in thine own act and valour
As thou art in desire? Wouldst thou have that
Which thou esteem'st the ornament of life
And live a coward in thine own esteem,
Letting 'I dare not' wait upon 'I would,'
Like a the poor cat i' the' adage.

She knows her husband's ego and his weakness: so
she questions his manhood, 'Art thou afeard?' She
also reminds him that it was he who first 'dressed'
himself in royal garments. And now he is like the cat
that wants the milk but is afraid to get its feet wet.
    She continues her attack on his manhood:

When you durst do it, you were a man;
And to be more than what you were, you would
Be so much more the man. Nor time nor place
Did then adhere, and yet you would make both.
They have made themselves, and that their fitness
    now
Does unmake you. I have given suck, and know
I would while it was smiling in my face,
Have plucked my nipple from his boneless gums
And dashed the brains out, had I so sworn as you
Have done to this.

Once more these have to be some of the most horrific
words ever spoken by a woman on the stage. First,

she taunts her husband for not being a man. Then in a startling confession, she says that if she had sworn to do something, she would keep her word even if it meant that she would have to 'pluck my nipple' from her suckling baby to be followed by dashing the baby's 'brains out'. What kind of woman is she? What kind of mother?

What has happened to Lady Macbeth? She has identified herself with the negative aspects of her animus. She has denied her womanhood and embraced what she believes are the qualities of a man. What qualities does she embrace? All that is negative, cruel and heartless. She denies her very selfhood as a woman to become the cruellest of men. This is what happens to a woman who embraces only the negative characteristics of a man. Can a man be cruel, ruthless, sadistic? Yes, for from the beginning of time man has been a fighter, and only over thousands of years has he learned to control the Darwinian traits that still lie dormant in the unconscious, traits that have been controlled by being civilised. But we know that at any time these dreadful traits can be released, the history of the twentieth century and the horrors of the Second World War are the only reminders we need know to understand that we must always be alert to our individual and collective shadow.

Macbeth is won over by his wife and will murder the king in his sleep. But how? Lady Macbeth has a plan, and Macbeth submits to it. He has allowed his shadow to overcome him. She has allowed her negative animus to overwhelm her. Are they evil people? We think not. By their reactions to the murder of King Duncan, we see that they basically were good people (evil people would have no remorse), but in a moment of blindness, they allowed themselves to become victims of their own dark powers. Before we end our discussion, let us examine their responses to the murder of Duncan.

Macbeth has returned to his wife. He has performed the deed, but he is in a state of shock. He feels a tremendous guilt for he has also murdered the king's grooms to make it seem their guilt. When he gapes at his bloody hands, he says, 'will all great Neptune's ocean wash this blood, clean from my hand? No, this my hand will rather, the multitudinous seas incarnadine, making the green one red.' And then the most damning comment, 'to know my deed 'twere best not to know myself'.

The latter comment is of utter importance from a psychological perspective. Macbeth, had he made an effort to know himself, to introspect, to analyse more carefully his inner self, could have avoided succumbing to his shadow. He allowed, however, the taunting of his wife to spur him on to regicide. Had he been a more confident man, a man who knew himself from a lifetime of self-examination, he would never have murdered Duncan. He should have allowed his murderous desires to remain in the light of his consciousness, to see them for what they were, and their horror would have horrified him, and he would not have lost his manhood to murder. It is not manly to murder, quite the opposite, murder transforms a human being into something nearly inhuman. He will never again experience a good night's sleep, 'Macbeth shall sleep no more.'

Lady Macbeth again is contemptuous of her husband's fear and trembling. When she sees that he has failed to leave the murder weapons with the grooms, she exhorts him to return and put them into their hands. But he will not return to that chamber of horrors. So she goes, and when she returns, her hands too have blood on them. She mocks her husband, 'a little water clears us of this deed', and yet she will suffer most for what she has done. She can never sleep securely again in the dark, always needing a lighted candle nearby. She obsessively wrings her hands as if to wash away the blood (and her guilt). She speaks one of the most famous lines in Shakespeare, 'Here's the smell of the blood still. All the perfumes of Arabia will not sweeten this little hand. O, O, O!'

The only cure for both Macbeth and his wife lies in religion, lies in God's forgiveness. And yet neither turns to God. Macbeth goes to his end fighting Macduff, and Lady Macbeth cannot any longer live with herself and commits suicide.

Two people, who were not evil, but performed evil because they would not listen to their consciences, two people who underestimated their own humanity, two people who had they actually embarked upon the inner journey, to become familiar with their shadow, their anima or animus, may have had the courage to refuse what their shadows insidiously urged them to do. Is it no wonder that sculpted into the stone of Greek temples are the words 'Know Thyself'. Such knowledge helps us to avoid the kind of tragedy that the Macbeths caused themselves, and the innocent others who were not only murdered but butchered, like Macduff's wife and children, his 'pretty ones'.

Notes

1 Jolande Jacobi, *The Way of Individuation*, trans. R. F. C. Hall (New York: New American Library, 1965), pp. 45–6.
2 Ibid., p. 39.

Questions for reflection on the anima

- Do I find myself (if male) often criticising for no reason women, family members, friends or colleagues?
- If I do, do I examine myself in order to understand what about myself I am projecting onto the opposite sex?
- Do I (if female) find myself too critical of men?
- If I do, do I examine myself for the cause of such negativity?
- Have I made an effort to record my dreams as a way of understanding my contra-sexual archetype, the anima or the animus?
- When I am depressed, do I find myself particularly critical of the opposite sex, and if I do, have I examined myself thoroughly enough to see that perhaps my perspective of the opposite sex may indeed have something to do with my depression?

Questions for reflections on the shadow

- When shadow ideas appear in my mind, do I too quickly repress them?
- Have I learned from Jung to analyse these ideas because they are aspects of my personality, and the more I own them, the more I will not project them onto other people? For instance, if I often accuse friends of being arrogant, then maybe I am guilty of such.

- Am I one of those people Christ warns us about, one who sees the splinter in another's eye but not the beam in my own?
- Again, am I recording my shadow dreams, keeping in mind that dreams are windows into the soul?
- Am I like Macbeth, who easily and quickly repressed the shadow into the unconscious?
- Do I understand that not only must the shadow be recognised and accepted, but also forgiven?
- Have I ever looked in the mirror at myself and said the words, 'I forgive you'?

4

Gerard Manley Hopkins and the 'Terrible Sonnets'

John Henry Cardinal Newman founded University College in Dublin, hoping to establish a college where Catholics could receive as fine an education as offered at Dublin's Trinity College, which refused to admit Catholics. One is amazed today that such discrimination could actually exist in Ireland's capital city. For many reasons, the college floundered, and Newman had to abandon it, handing it over to the Jesuits, well known throughout Europe as one of the finest teaching orders.

When University College needed a new Classics professor, several names were considered, including that of Gerard Manley Hopkins. Although he was not aware of it until he was appointed, Hopkins was not the first choice – far from it. The Jesuit order had concluded that he was an eccentric man, and his superiors had never taken him seriously. Hopkins, however, had been admired at Oxford as a brilliant scholar, dubbed the 'star of Balliol', its most gifted student. Because of Newman's influence, he embraced Catholicism and decided to become a priest. He had toyed with becoming a Benedictine, but in the end settled for the Society of Jesus, known as the 'soldiers of Christ' for the rigour of their intellectual, religious formation and their fierce apologetics.

At first, Hopkins was happy as a novice Jesuit. His days at St Beuno's in Wales were among the happiest times of his life, almost the equal of his joyful days spent as an undergraduate at Oxford. While living in Wales, Hopkins wrote his most ecstatic lyrical poetry, poems that today Hopkins aficionados know by heart: 'Pied Beauty', 'God's Grandeur' and 'The Windhover'. While at St Beuno's, at the recommendation of the Rector, Hopkins wrote his masterpiece *The Wreck of the Deutchland*, a poem fraught with a new, innovative idiom and rhythm. It was also a difficult poem to understand, and the Jesuit magazine refused to publish it, a disappointment with which Hopkins never truly came to terms.

Having failed several times as a parish priest, Hopkins was assigned by his superiors to the Classics department at Dublin's University College. In Dublin, a deep depression took hold of Hopkins.

Jung theorises that the first half of life is one during which the ego establishes itself in the outer world; it is a time of social position, marriage, parenthood and establishment of occupation. The second half of life is time devoted to a return to the inner journey, a time to re-evaluate the purpose of our life and to rededicate ourselves to spiritual values, a time when we look back on our life and decide if our goals have been successfully achieved. It is also a time to reflect on the imminence of death. The second half of life should also be a time of self-acceptance when a person can enjoy the full flowering of a life fully lived. When a person, however, realises that he or she may have not fully and authentically lived, then depression can rear its ugly head, dragging a person down into the roiling waters of the unconscious.

We can imagine Hopkins re-examining his life, a practice Jesuits had encouraged their members to do daily, and finding himself wanting. As a Jesuit, nothing had turned out to be successful, not even his

theological exam at St Beuno's, which he failed; not
his parish work, especially his work in the Glasgow
slums, whose squalor and degradation overwhelmed him; and certainly not his poetry, rejected
by his order and by his best friend, poet Robert
Bridges (future poet laureate of England), for its
obscurity. His lack of success on every level was
surely a blow to his ego.

When he arrived in Dublin, he was 40 years old, a
prime candidate for a mid-life crisis. In the midst of
his crisis, Hopkins wrenched from his gut the poems
commonly known as the 'terrible sonnets'. They
reveal a man naked in his pain, a man depressed,
lonely, lamenting his life, hovering at the edge of the
abyss of madness and self-destruction ('madness' is
a descriptive word he used in a letter to Robert
Bridges).

Why he had not succumbed to madness or suicide
is what today intrigues many people who read the
'terrible sonnets' – terrible because they are filled
with terror, agony, self-loathing and suicidal longing. In the first place, why, as a priest, is he despairing? Why depressed? Why suicidal? Hopkins was a
man of deep religious faith who had dedicated his
life to God as a Jesuit priest. Surely such a man finds
peace in God, for do not men and women, who have
sacrificed their lives for God, receive, if not worldly
rewards, then spiritual gifts: consolation, peace of
mind, equilibrium, serenity and grace?

What happened to Hopkins?

Some Hopkins scholars (for example Paul Mariani) claim that the terrible sonnets reflect Hopkins'
'dark night of the soul', part of a five-stage mystical
journey: awakening, purgation, illumination, dark
night of the soul, and union. During the 'dark night',
a mystic must endure God's absence (it can be a brief

time or one of many years as shown by Mother Teresa's experience, to be addressed later). Evelyn Underhill writes:

> This is the period of spiritual confusion and impotence, the last drastic purification of the whole character, the re-making of personality in accordance with the demands of the transcendent sphere, which is called by some mystics the Dark Night of the Soul, by others the 'spiritual death,' or 'purgation of the will'. Whatever the psychological causes which produce it, all mystics agree that this state constitutes a supreme moral crisis, in which the soul is finally cleansed of all attachments to selfhood, and utterly surrendered to the purposes of the Divine life. Spiritual man is driven from his old paradise, enters on a new period of struggle, must evolve 'another storey to his soul'.[1]

Close reading of Hopkins' sonnets, however, reveals that Hopkins was not a man who felt God's absence. He rails at God, he complains to God, he even whines to God, but God is as real and present to him as are his Irish students and colleagues at University College. His poems are not the product of a mystical 'dark night' or an absence of God in his life. Furthermore, Hopkins does not live between faith and doubt as the twentieth-century priest and poet, R. S. Thomas lived, composing verses in which he laments that God is seemingly no longer open to 'our lure', that is, our prayers and longing.

Hopkins never wrote verse layered with doubt about God's presence. He converted to Catholicism because he had fervently believed in the real presence of Christ in the tabernacle of every Catholic church, chapel, abbey and convent. It was the bedrock of his faith, remaining with him to the day of his death.

In the 'terrible sonnets', Hopkins feels not so much God's absence as God's 'unresponsiveness'. He feels that God had seemingly ignored his poems, his 'letters' sent to someone far away – the letters that have, no doubt, arrived (to God), but they remain unanswered. This lack of response breaks the heart of the sender because he intensely loves, his mind and soul fixed on the image of his divine Beloved – Jesus Christ. He feels, as any other rejected lover would, that life without a response from the Beloved is rendered meaningless. The end result, therefore, is depression punctuated by a constant, nagging question, 'Why go on?'

Most people cannot live without an expression of love: they need to be told they are loved, and they need to be touched. Such is the human condition.

Hopkins was touch-starved. He was a celibate, a state of life to which he remained steadfastly faithful to the end of his life. But living in Dublin he was physically and emotionally removed from all that he loved: his large family, his best friends and his beloved England. He lived among the Irish, most of whom loathed the English. He was literally a stranger in a strange land:

To seem the stranger lies my lot, my life
Among strangers. Father and mother dear,
Brothers and sisters are in Christ not near
And he my peace/my parting, sword and strife.

England, whose honour O all my heart woos, wife
To my creating thought, would neither hear

Me, were I pleading, plead nor do I: I wear-
Y of idle a being but by where wars are rife.

I am in Ireland now; now I am at a third
Remove. Not but in all removes I can
Kind love both give and get. Only what word

Wisest my heart breeds dark heaven's baffling ban
Bars or hell's spell thwarts. This to hoard unheard,
Heard unheeded, leaves me a lonely began.

This sonnet is revelatory because Hopkins is a
stranger in several ways, but the most important
estrangement is that he is estranged from himself. As
someone depressed, he is not in touch with his Self.
This feeling of being a stranger had long been with
him, perhaps for a lifetime. Let us examine the prob-
able cause.

There has lately been much scholarly speculation
about Hopkins' sexuality. If he was a homosexual, as
his major biographers have indicated (Paddy Kitchens, Robert Bernard Martin), then he is indeed a
stranger in a world where to be homosexual is
'strange' and must be hidden because it is viewed as
deviant (particularly in Victorian England). And of
course, he is now living 'among strangers', the Irish.
Keep in mind that Hopkins is a graduate of one of the
British Empire's finest colleges, Oxford. He is from
the upper-middle class. His English accent is that of
an Oxford aesthete, which in Ireland would be something despised. He is estranged from all the people
he loves: 'Father and mother dear / Brothers and sisters are in Christ not near.' Observe that Hopkins
describes his family as not 'in Christ' near. His belief
is that as a Catholic he is closer to Christ because he is
a member of the one, true Catholic faith. In the nine-

teenth century the idea of *extra ecclesiam nulla salus* –
no salvation outside the Church – had been a belief
held by Catholics; it was also the teaching of the
Church at that time. When Hopkins converted to
Catholicism, to the chagrin of his friends and family,
he hastened his acceptance into Mother Church
because he firmly believed that his immortal soul
was in danger.

Is his conflicted sexuality and familial and
national estrangement enough to cause a person to
be depressed? More than enough. As we have seen,
Jung says that we all wear personae (masks), and we
identify with the masks we wear; we often identify
so much with our masks that we lose contact with the
true Self that lies beneath the mask. What are the
masks with which Hopkins is identifying? He is a
son and he is a brother. In the first half of life, we
separate from our parents and develop a strong,
world-oriented ego. Hopkins seems not to have been
able to renounce his youthful identifications, a form
of arrested development. He is still attached to his
birth mother as well as to Mother England. His projections upon people and a nation do not allow Hopkins to take a hold of his life, do not allow the
flowering of self-realisation. He cannot become himself as long as he identifies with these youthful projections. If he could clearly see himself in his new role
as a professor and accept the locus of his new position, he could rise above his depression. If he could
embrace himself, including the self he has hidden
from the world (his sexual self), he would become a
more integrated, whole human being.

In the second stanza, Hopkins describes England
as his wife. He woos her as a lover would a woman.
This identification, as a lover, is an odd one because
Hopkins is a priest, thus a chaste man. As a poet he

must produce (not reproduce): his offspring are his poems. But during his time in Ireland, he produces little verse of quality. In another poem, he describes himself as a eunuch: emasculated, he feels that he will never again be able to produce poems.

Without touch, without human love, without self-acceptance, a stranger to himself and to Ireland, Hopkins comes close to self-slaughter as expressed in the following 'terrible sonnet', 'Carrion Comfort':

Not, I'll not, carrion comfort, Despair, not feast on
  thee;
Not untwist – slack they may be – these last
  strands of man
In me or, most weary, cry I can no more I can;
Can something, hope, wish day come, not choose
  not to be.

But ah, but O thou terrible, why wouldst thou
  rude on me
Thy wring-world right foot rock? lay a lionlimb
  against me? scan
With darksome devouring eyes my bruisèd bones?
  and fan
O in turns of tempest, me heaped there; me frantic
  to avoid thee and flee?

Why? That my chaff might fly; my grain lie, sheer
  and clear.
nay in all that toil, that coil, since (seems) I kissed
  the rod,
Hand rather, my heart lo! lapped strength, stole
  joy, would laugh, chéer.

Cheer whom though? The hero whose
  heave-handling flung me, fóot tród

Me? or me that fought him? O which one? is it
    each one? That night, that year
Of now done darkness I wretch lay wrestling with
    (my God!) my God.

We hear the echo of Hamlet's soliloquy, 'To be or not
to be', in his words 'not choose not to be', Hamlet's
words a meditation on suicide. Hopkins struggles
not to succumb to suicide; it is a fight, a struggle, a
wrestling whose result remains uncertain. Yet in the
end, Hopkins chooses to be: to live. How did he win
his combat against despair? I believe he survived
through his creative outlet: poetry. The poem
becomes his 'confessional box', the formal structure
of the sonnet, into which he pours his inner turmoil,
where he tries to order his life, to make sense of it,
and paradoxically render it beautiful; therefore, the
pathos of the terrible sonnets reminds one of the
terrible beauty of Greek tragedies. The poem also
serves, in modern terminology, as a therapist: the
poem absorbs the poet's articulation of his inner
pains (a kind of transference); the poem does not
judge him, for like a good therapist it listens, allowing the poet himself to achieve insight about himself.
The best therapists are those who attentively listen
and who are rarely didactic, perhaps asking a wise
question here and there to lead the patient to his own
answers about his problems.

  Capturing his spiritual/psychological state of
being in verse is similar to a cathartic experience for
Hopkins, yet he remained a lonely man craving
human touch, a man hungry for another reader of his
poems (his poetry was published posthumously in
the twentieth century by his friend, Robert Bridges),
hungry for someone to understand his new, innova-

tive but difficult-to-understand verse. Or to put it another way: he longed for someone to understand *him*!

How does this explication fit in with Jungian theory. I turn now to one of our finest Jungian experts, Father Josef Goldbrunner. He writes:

> In most neuroses the 'natural soul' is buried. Our Christian education, our asceticism and striving for perfection tend all too much to repress and eliminate the natural soul. There is still no affirmation of our total human nature, the deeper levels of the soul are still excluded from Christian penetration. The defection from the Church in the West is not merely a rejection of Christian faith; it is partly due to a feeling that the Church does not accept the whole of human nature, that inside the Church the deeper levels of the personality cannot breath and live.[2]

Christians today have an advantage over a person like Hopkins because we have access to the knowledge that depth psychology offers us, one that leads to an acceptance of the wholeness of a person. Today we understand the danger of Platonic, dualistic thinking, one that divides a person in half: body and soul, with the body being the 'bad' partner and the soul the good (see Plato's dialogue, *Phaedrus*). Incarnational theology reminds us that the body and all its needs and desires are from God; therefore, they are not evil or irrational. Christ himself came to us *in carna*, in the flesh. Thus, our body is indeed, as St Paul reminds us, a temple of God: 'Do you not know that your body is a temple of the Holy Spirit within you, whom you have from God, and that you are not your own? For you have been purchased at a price. Therefore glorify God in your body' (1 Cor. 6:19).

Hopkins, however, was a product of the nineteenth century, and the Catholicism he embraced was more aligned to that of the twelfth century. Hopkins could have sat at the table with a medieval Catholic priest or monk and felt quite at home, both believing in the same church dogmas and teachings, still practising the same rituals and liturgies – the Mass in Latin, receiving the same sacraments, and amassing indulgences. Being denied the fruit of the next century's newest science, psychology, Hopkins suffered much from shame – ashamed of being Gerard Manley Hopkins, of his sexual nature – and yet his poetry, journals and letters reveal that he had led a blameless life. He surely believed that he abided in a state of grace. But this knowledge does not nullify his feelings of shame, for I firmly believe that he knew that his sexual orientation fell under the infamous, timeworn expression, 'The love that dare not speak its name.' For confirmation of this belief, one need only read his poetry, particularly 'Epithalamion', his journals and his letters. Furthermore, Hopkins was too introspective a man, one who explored his inner landscape, not to know himself and his desires.

About shame, Jane Polden writes:

> Shame is what we feel when we fail to live up to our ego ideal. The ego ideal is the name given by psychoanalysis to describe the self's conception of how it wants to see itself, formed through identification with parental views about what is expected of us, if we are to deserve love and approval. Initially our ego

> ideals are based upon our parents' values, but as we mature they expand to include wider cultural values. While guilt comes from concern that we may hurt others, shame is anchored in the fear that others will think badly of us and reject us, and it is shame rather than guilt that informs many of the depressive's self-reproaches.[3]

How does a Catholic priest of the nineteenth century face his 'shameful' sexual orientation? If he is true to his Church's teachings, then he accepts the fact that he is, according to the Church's teaching, unnatural; therefore, he must be constantly vigilant to keep his 'unnatural' (thus perverse) self in check. Imagine the psychic energy involved in doing so. Hopkins' most often used ascetical exercise was 'custody of the eyes', when he would not allow himself to gaze upon mortal or natural beauty, offering it as a sacrifice to God. Flagellating the body had been a common practice in most religious orders (disciplining the black horse of Plato's charioteer), one that flowed into the twentieth century. Custody of the eyes is psychic or spiritual flagellation, its practice pathological, whose psychic and spiritual harm incalculable.

In the second stanza, Hopkins feels that his Lord is being 'terrible' to him; he feels that his Lord is being 'rude' by kicking him as a lion would, out to devour him. These are frightening images, and Hopkins feels that his very life is at stake. Even the eyes of the lion are 'darksome devouring eyes' watching with avidity his bruised bones.

Verses in the second quatrain are all posed as questions. They can be summarised by one general question: 'Why have you so brutalized me, abandoning me alone in a heap upon a field so frightened that

I must do all I can to avoid you?' This is such a heart-rending question to come from a holy priest who is now imagining his adversary to be God himself, who treats him abominably for reasons he cannot fathom.

We, his readers, cannot help being moved by his poignant questions. Like him, we are completely confused as to why Hopkins has been nearly kicked to death by a 'right foot rock' and opposed by 'a lionlimb against me'. It is as if he has been mauled by some huge, voracious animal as he now lies alone in a heap with tempestuous winds blown over him, similar to those of Shakespeare's King Lear.

In the sestet, a bewildered Hopkins tries to understand why he is being so brutally punished. He is completely flummoxed because he has been an obedient follower: 'I kissed the rod/Hand rather, my heart lo! Lapped strength, stole joy, would laugh, cheer.' But like winnowed (beaten) chaff he is blown away to who knows where. He concludes that he is merely a wretch who has wrestled 'with (my God!) my God'.

Hopkins' prior descriptions of Christ both in poetry and in his sermons do not support this conclusion, that Christ is the adversary. Hopkins wants to believe that God and he are wrestling, as opposed to a life-and-death duel, because it then transforms his defeat into a lovers' quarrel. This analogy is merely an escape mechanism: Hopkins is prostrate by depression; he has been brutalised by his own archetypal shadow. His shadow has 'wrestled' him to the ground because the shadow represents those things about ourselves we would rather not face or accept; thus, we repress them into the unconscious that is attempting to force Hopkins to face aspects of himself that he has been fleeing from and avoiding.

One could perhaps view 'Carrion Comfort' as a triumphant poem: Hopkins is still alive, still writing poems. Perhaps he chose life over death because of poetry, which proves to be an outlet for his inner agony. Is it not a truism that most great art is the result of great suffering?

The 'terrible sonnets' chronicle Hopkins' battle with himself, a combat between the two horses of body and soul, one that came to a head at mid-life when he was teaching at University College in Dublin. Jane Polden writes:

> The dramas of mid-life are dramas of abandonment and freedom, of highly charged sexual engagement in real time or in fantasy, and sudden encounters with mortality and loss. It is a time when everything – from the most fundamental questions of identity and meaning, to the daily experience of our own bodies and sexuality – is thrown into upheaval, making mid-life transition for many people the most disturbing period of life since the onset of adolescence.[4]

Here is Hopkins' mid-life description of his psychic landscape in 'No worst, there is none',

O the mind has mountains; cliffs of fall
Frightful, sheer, no-man fathomed. Hold them
   cheap
May who ne'er hung there. Nor does long our small
Durance deal with that steep or deep. Here I creep,
Wretch, under a comfort serves in a whirlwind: all
Life death does end and each day dies with sleep.

He sees himself as a wretch, and the only release from his wretchedness is either death or sleep; any kind of unconsciousness is preferred over consciousness. In a mid-life crisis, Jung says, the unconscious does its best to stir the psychic waters, its purpose to spur the ego to embark upon the inner journey, and finally to address the archetypal shadow.

Where, then, could the poet turn? He can only do what he has always done before: be patient and pray: 'Patience, hard thing! The hard thing but to pray' (poem 68).

To a Jesuit priest in the nineteenth century, as well as today, everything comes down to prayer, and through it he won a priceless diamond of wisdom. He learned that even as one can have compassion for others who suffer and sin, he can also express compassion for himself:

> My own heart let me more have pity on; let
> Me live to my sad self hereafter kind,
> Charitable; not live this tormented mind
> With this tormented mind tormenting yet.

To achieve a smidgen of peace of mind, he has to cease from tormenting himself to be something he cannot be. Pity for himself, and self-acceptance, is his only cure. Along with his poetic outlet, it is his only viable means of self-preservation: self-acceptance is self-preservation. Through God's grace and his efforts to be Christ-like, he somehow finds within himself the pity and compassion to survive and to endure.

Primary Text

W. H. Gardner and N. H. MacKenzie (eds), *The Poems of Gerard Manley Hopkins* (London: Oxford University Press, 1967).

Notes

1 Evelyn Underhill, *The Mystic Way* (London: J. M. Dent & Sons, 1913), p. 55.
2 Josef Goldbrunner, *Holiness is Wholeness* (New York: Pantheon Books, 1955), pp. 30–1.
3 Jane Polden, *Regeneration: Journey through the Mid-Life Crisis* (London: Continuum, 2002), p. 244.
4 Polden, *Regeneration*, back cover.

Questions for reflection

- What can Hopkins teach me about self-acceptance?
- Have I an outlet for my inner self, as Hopkins had with his poetry?
- Am I honest with myself about sexuality, or have I, like Hopkins, avoided it?
- Am I happy in my job, or have I perhaps remained in an occupation that I do not particularly enjoy?
- In general, have I met my goals as a person?
- Can I describe myself as a whole person?
- If not, what in particular should I do to become whole?

- Am I praying enough?
- Am I putting time aside for introspection?
- What is the most important lesson I can learn from what I have just learned about Hopkins?

5

T. S. Eliot: The Despair of The Waste Land to the Hope of the Four Quartets

As a young man T. S. Eliot was haunted by a sense of guilt, primarily sexual guilt, and plagued by self-disgust. He was sensitive to the power of evil in the world, overwhelmed by the futility, emptiness and sterility of the twentieth century, especially the years between the two great wars, a time imbued with a spiritual malaise that seeped into his very soul, causing him to be a constant victim of depression. If it had been possible, Eliot would have fled to the desert like the Desert Fathers, for he believed the modern world to be corrupted. Thus, like Thomas Merton, he had developed deep-rooted *contemptus mundi*, that is, a contempt for the world. In fact, his biographer Lyndall Gordon compared Eliot's sensibility to that of Merton. In her two-volume biography, she writes:

> The monk, Thomas Merton, tried to explain their point of view (Desert Fathers). Solitaries, he said, regard the world as a wreck and are helpless to do good so long as they flounder among the wreckage. Their first obligation is to find a solid foothold and then to pull others to safety after them.[1]

Eliot was very much interested in how to live life. As a student, he majored in philosophy, but while visit-

ing Paris he decided that writing poetry would
become his vocation in life.

Eliot viewed the modern world with its lack of
direction, of values, faith and morals, and its destruc-
tiveness as a wasteland; thus his most famous poem
would be called *The Waste Land*. For someone who
viewed the world so negatively there was only one
place where he could turn for peace and solace: the
Church.

In the Church of England, Eliot found a solid foot-
hold. He converted and was baptised on 29 June 1927
in the small village church of Finstock in Oxford-
shire. His conversion was not a complete shock to
those who knew him well, although some friends
and many of his readers felt that he had betrayed
them by defecting to religion. Eliot's lifelong study of
mysticism began when he was a Harvard undergraduate. His notes (housed at Harvard) from his
college years (1908–14) reveal an extensive reading
list of the mystics. Records at Harvard's Houghton
Library show that Eliot borrowed over thirty books
on mysticism, including ones by such authorities as
Dean Inge, William James and Evelyn Underhill.
Eliot also read Eastern mysticism: he studied both
the Bhagavad Gita and the Upanishads. Allusions to
both Eastern and Western mysticism appear
throughout Eliot's poetry, beginning with *The Waste
Land* and continuing through to the *Four Quartets*;
similar allusions are evident in several of his plays,
most notably *Murder in the Cathedral* and *The Cocktail
Party*.

The mature Eliot was very much drawn to the
mystics of the late Middle Ages and especially to the
'via negativa' of St John of the Cross, incorporating
the Catholic mystic's actual words as his epigraph to
Sweeney Agonistes, 'Hence the Soul cannot be pos-

sessed by the divine union, until it has divested itself of the love of created beings.' He claims St John of the Cross more extensively in the *Four Quartets*, advocating the saint's mystical regimen as a means towards liberation from the ego.

Later, Eliot moved away from an attraction towards the ascetic Spanish mystic St John to a love for the compassionate, optimistic English four-teenth-century mystic Julian of Norwich. Eliot was so spiritually uplifted by her *Revelations of Divine Love*, he included verbatim her famous promise, 'All manner of thing shall be well', in the last movement of the fourth quartet, 'Little Gidding'. He desperately needed her message of hope and love during the dark night of the Second World War.

If *The Waste Land* is an autobiographical account of Eliot's despair, in detail describing his barrenness, futility, lethargy and hopelessness, then his *Four Quartets* is an account of his new-found faith, hope and joy. Eliot wrote his four movements in homage to Beethoven's last quartets:

> I have long aimed to write poetry, to write poetry ... so transparent that we should not see the poetry, but that which we are meant to see through poetry ... to get beyond poetry, as Beethoven, in his later works strove to get beyond music.[2]

As a composer develops a melodic line, Eliot takes several themes, introduces them (Exposition) in the first movement, varies them (Development) in the second movement, expands them (Amplification) in the third movement, and offers a denouement (Recapitulation) in the last movement. Each quartet is divided into five sections, within which themes are in contrapuntal relation to each other, one rising as the other declines.

Why the quartet, rather than some other musical form? If we accept Carl Jung's definition of quaternity as being symbolic of wholeness or completeness, then we can appreciate that Eliot's *Four Quartets* serves as his poetic and spiritual summation, achieved when Eliot was in his full maturity, at the height of his poetic powers.

For the sake of clarity, let us define quarternity:

> The quaternity is one of the most widespread archetypes and has also proved to be one of the most useful schemata for representing the arrangement of the functions by which the conscious mind takes its bearings. It is like the crossed threads in the telescope of our understanding. The cross formed by the points of the quaternity is no less universal and has in addition the highest possible moral and religious significance for Western man.[3]

Let us now, in more detail, access Eliot's psychological profile. What kind of young man was Eliot. Intellectually he was a brilliant scholar, and at Harvard he had the opportunity to study with some of its legendary philosophers, George Palmer, George Santayana and William James. To understand what kind of young man Eliot was, we need only read his autobiographical *The Love Song of J. Alfred Prufrock*. Prufrock was a man laden with fear, self-doubt and melancholy. He in no way could be described as a joyful man. According to Jung's theory of types, Eliot would fall under the description of introvert with thinking his dominant personality function. In the poem, Prufrock (Eliot) longs for love, longs to reach out to a woman, longs to connect, but he cannot because he is paralysed by fear and self-consciousness. He notices everything about women, down to the hair on their arms. But the question that haunts him is 'Do I dare?' He is unable to dare to speak to another, to disturb the habitual, safe universe he has created for himself. In fact, he is so fearful and self-conscious that he would not dare eat a peach in public.

His fear renders him a man depressed, the type of man who prefers to go out in the night and wander the streets. He chooses to walk in the more sordid neighbourhoods of the cities where he lives. When he lived in Paris, he stood in darkened doorways watching prostitutes and others involved in their shady dealings.

We can infer that Eliot is drawn to such places because he cannot integrate his own instinctual drives. He is afraid of his own sexuality, likely the result of his early rearing in a Puritanical family, from which he could only free himself by a drastic step, moving to live permanently in England. During the individuation process, there must be a clean break from our parents in order to allow ourselves to develop our own autonomy, our own selves.

Employing Prufrock as a persona, Eliot speaks like a man in his forties. He longs to feel young again (Eliot was only in his twenties when the poem was published in 1917), and would like to be daring by walking along a beach with his white flannels rolled up. But being so identified with being a gentleman, he cannot remove the persona and be freely himself.

His persona of a middle-aged man correlates with Eliot's philosophical bent of mind. Eliot is a thinker; he seeks the meaning of life, but he finds no sufficient philosophy to explain his own depression which he projects onto every city he visits; thus Boston, Paris and London are always described in drab, grey colours, the sun rarely shining. Even philosophy frightens him, admitting his fear to ask the deep, overwhelming questions. Then his sense of inferiority takes over. He demeans himself by mocking himself: he is not a prophet, he is not a tragic hero like Hamlet, only a man afraid. He sees himself as lower than the crawling crabs of the sea, and further describes himself as obtuse, ridiculous, cautious and foolish.

When a man is filled with such self-loathing, is it any wonder that he suffers from depression?

What did Eliot actually want in life? His biographer indicates that Eliot truly wanted to be perfect; in fact, he wanted to be a saint. We are reminded that Thomas Merton wished for the same thing. It came to Merton that to become a saint was his reason for being when his best friend Robert Lax said that becoming a saint should be Merton's goal, now that he had converted to Catholicism. Merton would eventually learn how unrealistic his goal was, and that the best way to live was simply to be oneself and let God do the rest.

Eliot's desire for perfection manifested itself early in his life, around the time he graduated from Harvard. His biographer writes:

> About the same time that Eliot graduated from Harvard College, while walking one day in Boston, he saw the streets suddenly shrink and divide. His everyday preoccupations, his past, all the claims of the future fell away and he was enfolded in a great silence. In June 1910 he wrote a poem he never published called

'Silence', his first and perhaps most lucid description of the timeless moment ... At the age of twenty-one Eliot had one of those experiences which, he said, many have had once or twice in their lives and been unable to put into words. 'You may call it communion with the Divine or you may call it temporary crystallization of the mind', he said on another occasion. For some such a moment is part of an orthodox religious life ... For Eliot, however, the memory of bliss was to remain a kind of torment, a mocking reminder through the years that followed that there was an area of experience just beyond his grasp, which contemporary images could not compass.[4]

To become a saint means to take upon oneself the goal of perfection. We already know that such a goal for a human being is an impossible one, one that leads to constant frustration and finally to depression. For Eliot it led to a nervous breakdown in 1921, while he was living and working in London. While recuperating in France, Eliot worked on his spiritual autobiography, which is how he viewed *The Waste Land* at the time. Such a description (spiritual autobiography) he would later abandon, due to the influence of Ezra Pound who edited the whole of *The Waste Land*, excising many parts of the poem until it became *The Waste Land* we now have. There is much debate today about whether or not Eliot should have handed over his poem to Pound. We shall never know whether or not Eliot's poem as he originally composed it would have achieved the enormous success it achieved under Pound's influence, which at the time was ubiquitous in London literary circles. Eliot met all the important artists of the time, including its leading female intellectual, Virginia Woolf, the controlling centre of the Bloomsbury Group.

The Waste Land is really a description of Eliot's soulscape, an effective example of what Jung calls psychological projection. Eliot critic Nancy Hargrove writes:

> *The Waste Land* is the apex of Eliot's early poetry. Significantly, the technique of using urban landscape as symbol reaches its high point here. In the poem Eliot presents the full horror of a civilization that has rejected both human and divine love and that consequently is physically, emotionally, and spiritually sterile. Eliot's first choice for the epigraphy was the agonized death cry of Joseph Conrad's Kurtz, 'The horror! The horror!' and this cry echoes and re-echoes in every terrifying scene in *The Waste Land.*[5]

He had not yet converted to the Church of England. He was still a modern man in search of a soul. He had no financial security or an occupation in which he took relish. He felt dissatisfied with his personal life and with life in general. He had, however, one outlet: his poetry. Thus, he pours himself into *The Waste Land*, all of his fears, anxieties, doubts, tribulations, hopes and desires. But it all truly comes down to what is missing in his life: perfection. He has made no progress in becoming the perfect man he had hoped to become. The result of the dawning of this realisation is a nervous breakdown.

What would a Jungian therapist say to a man like Eliot? She would counsel him to accept himself as he is. She would encourage him to continue to write poetry and to have it published, for it would fortify

Eliot's ego, one that too often made Eliot feel like a failure. A brilliant man, Eliot could only secure a lowly job at a London bank. Jung would also advise him to be more gentle with himself, to forgive himself for what he perceives as his failures (and in theological terminology, sins). Failure at anything, at games, at work, marriage, friendship, parenting, all can cause a person to become depressed. Jung would also advise Eliot to come to terms with his disgust of sexuality, to see it as it should be seen, as a healthy, holy part of life. Jung would also encourage a person with a spiritual inclination to pursue it. Eliot is only a few years away from his conversion in 1927. When he finally turns to God and prayer, he turns his life around for the good. His biographer writes:

> Self-transformation begins from what precedes it: a person who feels weak, helpless, and locked in fears: on the one hand, fear of action; on the other, fear of inaction. Behind these lurks a greater fear of the unknown.[6]

We have looked at Eliot's life, drawing from his pre-conversion poetry a portrait of an artist as a young man. For the most part, he is sad and depressed. He undergoes one tremendous risk, he marries. Unfortunately his marriage is a disaster (because of his inadequacy and her psychosis), tossing him into greater depression. It is enough for us to know that Eliot has a while to go before he wins happiness and peace of soul. So let us now make a huge leap and look at the man who wrote one of the greatest religious plays of the twentieth century, *Murder in the Cathedral*.

Eliot may not ever be able to become a saint, but there is nothing to prevent him from writing a play about one – St Thomas à Becket. His biographer writes:

> He (Eliot) was simply too clever to be a saint. In his duality as warped saint, Eliot was the epitome of twentieth-century extremism. Yet his struggle to subdue intellectual pride, fury, and hatred proved fertile matter for poetry. There remains the paradox of a man who wished to be a saint above poet but who became all the greater as a poet for his failure to attain sainthood. He fell back on another goal, to be God's agent.[7]

Eliot becomes God's agent in his powerful, inspiring Christian play about the martyrdom of Thomas Becket. What the play essentially concerns is the murder of Thomas Becket, the Archbishop of Canterbury, appointed to his position by Henry II. Henry thought he could get more control of the rich and powerful Catholic Church if he assigned his good friend and fellow libertine to the most powerful religious position in England. Becket warned Henry not to do it, but the king ignored the warning. Becket, in a complete about-face, found God, and devoted himself to God's Church here on earth.

On a literal level, the play may be about twelfth-century English history and the battle between Henry II and Becket, but on a symbolic level it is the story of a man who finds his soul, mirroring T. S. Eliot's search for soul.

Eliot began writing the play in 1935, eight years after his conversion. By this time Eliot had concluded that only a living faith and a reaching out for God gave meaning to life. He often attended Mass, and he prayed daily. When the opportunity presented itself in the form of a request from the Friends of Canterbury Cathedral to write a play for their annual festival, Eliot grabbed it.

The play's real purpose is to express Eliot's religious beliefs, but it also serves as an exploration of several relationships: between spiritual and civil authority, common people and their civil and spiritual leaders, between a man, king, church and God. It is also an exploration of the meaning of martyrdom. Eliot poses two important questions: What is a martyr? And, who makes a martyr?

In trying to answer those two questions, Eliot is able to be didactic in a marvellous Christmas homily preached by Becket, who is really expressing the radiant gist of Eliot's spirituality. In short, Eliot believes that a Christian offers himself body and soul to God. A Christian holds nothing back from God, not even his life. His whole life is in God's hands; thus a practising Christian has no problem with Christ's prayer to God the Father, 'Not my will but Thine be done.' For this is exactly how Becket lives his last days: he knows an attempt will be made upon his life, but he does nothing to stop it. He continues to live his life as a priest, celebrating Mass at the same altar and at the same time as he always had. Thus, Henry's knights know full well where and when to find him and to murder him.

As a priest, when Becket raises up the host and the chalice to God, he is holding up Christ to God. Christ again is to be sacrificed. Christ again is to be a martyr. Christ again is offered as the redeemer of the world. But at the same time, Becket is offering himself to God. He offers his ego, his selfhood to God to do with them what he will. Becket is a man in imitation of Christ.

Again Becket could describe himself with St Paul's words 'Not I, but Christ within me' (Gal. 2:20). This is the goal of human individuation in the West: to realise the archetypal Christ within. Josef Goldbrunner writes:

> Even Christ Himself can become the unifying symbol (of the individual). According to Jung, Paul expresses this in the words, 'I live, yet not I, but Christ lives in me.' As a unifying symbol, Christ the 'corner-stone' is at the same time the stone of wisdom in which everything is contained. That alone is the reason for the influence of Christianity: 'The apparently unique life of Christ has become the hallowed symbol because it is the psychological prototype of the only meaningful life ... of a life which strives to attain the individual, that is to say, the absolute and unconditional realization of the law peculiar to itself.' (Jung) Christ remained faithful unto death to the inner law which was inborn in Him. Therefore He is the supreme example of the process of becoming a personality.[8]

Becket becomes his true Self by obeying his inner law. T. S. Eliot also became himself by obeying his inner law. The confused young man we met in *The Love Song of J. Alfred Prufrock*, the man who suffered a nervous breakdown while writing *The Waste Land*, the poet who wrote *The Hollow Men*, became the joyful Christian who was able to compose one of the greatest plays of the twentieth century, a play that is imbued with the message of Christ, 'In losing yourself you will find yourself.'

In his last years, Eliot had a happy marriage and religious serenity. His last critical work addressed the life and work of the metaphysical poet George Herbert. Lyndall Gordon ends her essay with the following poem, about which Eliot's biographer says, 'Eliot closes by quoting in full the poem "Love", in which every line suggests a parallel with Eliot's own life':[9]

Love
Love bade me welcome, yet my soul drew back
Guilty of dust and sin
Buy quick-eyed Love, observing me grow slack
From my first entrance in,
Drew nearer to me, sweetly questioning,
If I lack'd any thing.

'A guest,' I answer'd, 'worthy to be here';
Love said, 'You shall be he.'
'I the unkind, ungrateful? Ah, my deare,
I cannot look on thee.'
Love took my hand, and smiling did reply,
'Who made the eyes but I?'

'Truth, Lord, but I have marr'd them: let my shame
Go where it doth deserve.'
'And know you not,' says Love, 'who bore the
    blame?'
'My deare, then I will serve.'
'You must sit down,' says Love, 'and taste my meat.'
So I did sit and eat.

Notes

1   Lyndall Gordon, *Eliot's Early Years* (London: Oxford University Press, 1977), p. 122.
2   Lyndall Gordon, *Eliot's New Life* (New York: Farrar, Straus & Giroux, 1988), p, 123.
3   Daryl Sharp, *C. G. Jung: A Primer of Terms and Concepts* (Toronto: Inner City Books, 1991), p. 110.
4   Gordon, *Eliot's Early Years*, p. 17.
5   Nancy Duvall Hargrove, *Landscape as Symbol in the Poetry of T. S. Eliot* (Jackson: University Press of Misissippi, 1978), p. 61.
6   Lyndall Gordon, *T. S. Eliot: An Imperfect Life* (New York: W. W. Norton & Co., 1998), p. 210.
7   Gordon, *An Imperfect Life*, p. 53.
8   Josef Goldbrunner, *Individuation* (Notre Dame, IN: University of Notre Dame Press, 1964), p. 154.
9   Gordon, *An Imperfect Life*, p. 524.

Questions for reflection

- Have I realised yet the inspirational power of poetry?
- Have I read Eliot, now realising that he caught in both his verse and prose the spiritual malaise of modern times, and that I perhaps may find in his work aspects of myself?
- From the little I have just read about Eliot, is there anything he can teach me about depression and spirituality?
- Eliot had a great love of the Mass, which helped him in his times of depression. Can I make an effort to attend Mass more than once a week?

- Have I ever thought of the possibility of capturing my own soulscape in writing poetry?
- During times of depression, Eliot found great peace in the fourteenth-century mystic Lady Julian of Norwich. Have I ever read her? If not, then perhaps I should become acquainted with her by reading her classic *Revelations of Divine Love*.

6

Henri Nouwen's Nervous Breakdown

In his diaries, Nouwen candidly writes about depression. Having become a famous priest and lecturer, Nouwen had travelled all over the world and touched many people. But there was a void in his life, one caused by his low self-esteem and his propensity to demand so much attention from his friends. When his demands were not met, he fell into deep depressions.

At L'Arche Daybreak in Toronto where Nouwen had become a pastor to the handicapped, Nouwen met a young assistant, Nathan Ball. They became very close friends, so close that Nouwen made Nathan the centre of his emotional stability.[1] He writes:

> Among my many friends, one had been able to touch me in a way I had never been touched before. Our friendship encouraged me to allow myself to be loved and cared for with greater trust and confidence. It was a totally new experience for me, and it brought me immense joy and peace. It seemed as if a door of my interior life had been opened, a door that remained locked during my youth and most of my adult life.[2]

However, Nouwen's great need for love and affection frightened Ball, and he backed off. Believing the friendship had ended, Nouwen suffered a nervous breakdown. He confesses in his beautiful book, *The Inner Voice of Love*:

> This deeply satisfying friendship became the road to my anguish, because I soon discovered the enormous space that had been opened for me could not be filled by the one who had opened it. I became possessive, needy, and dependent, and when the friendship finally had to be interrupted, I fell apart. I felt abandoned, rejected, and betrayed. Indeed, the extremes touched each other.[3]

Nouwen entered deep therapy; part of the healing process involved therapists holding Nouwen in a non-sexual way. He would be fully clothed on a bed, and there he would be held as one would hold a frightened child; his therapists encouraged him to express his repressed feelings, to weep, to scream, to writhe as they, like loving parents, consolingly caressed him.

He also found release for his pent-up emotions in writing, for it was during this time he wrote *The Inner Voice of Love*, a candid spiritual confession and an inspiring account of his breakdown and recovery. Nouwen's falling in love with Nathan Ball was perhaps the best thing that could have happened to him. It made him face who he was, enabling him to free himself emotionally, to realise that he was human like the rest of us. Nouwen summarises his experience:

> I have moved through anguish to freedom, through depression to peace, through despair to hope. It certainly was a time of purification

for me. My heart, ever questioning, my goodness, value, and worth, has become anchored
in a deeper love and thus less dependent on
the praise and blame of those around me. It
also has grown into a greater ability to give
love without always expecting love in return.[4]

As a priest Nouwen was permitted to love the Christ
in all people. And he did it so well. But to love
another human being, with both body and soul, was
a love forbidden him; thus, he accepted what he
initially devoted his life to, what he calls our First
Love: God. Any other kind of love was, as he
described it, a Second Love: human love. This divi-
sion of love into First and Second, however, is a poor
rationalisation: when we love another person, we at
the same time love God, 'Not I, but Christ in me.'
There is no duality.

I remember attending a talk given by Henri Nouwen at St Paul's Church, near Harvard, during the
1970s. What I remember most about him was his
riveting presence, how he emotionally reached out to
his audience, how he gesticulated with his large
hands that seemed to want to touch everyone
present.

A month later I was browsing in a Cambridge
bookstore. I happened to notice a man wearing a
beret, looked closer and recognised Henri Nouwen. I
wanted so much to go up to him and thank him for
his wonderful talk, but I was too shy. To this day I
regret not having talked to him.

The first of his books to impress me was his *Genesee
Diary*, one that put him on the map. It was a diary of
his time spent living the life of a Trappist monk at
Genesee Abbey in New York. Nouwen had been a

great admirer of Thomas Merton; he also hoped that he could emulate Merton's life as a Trappist monk.

His diary is a frank confession that the life of a contemplative monk was not for him. I much admired his naked, transparent style of writing: he presents himself warts and all. He also writes eloquently about his bouts of depression, the result of his deep-rooted need for people, and his hunger for acceptance from everyone.

As a diarist, he is far more open and accessible than Merton. Merton held much back, Nouwen held nothing back: he strips off all masks, and we see him as he struggles for seven months at Genesee. He writes of his disagreement with the abbot over the distribution of Holy Communion. Nouwen offered the transubstantiated host to anyone who came forward for it. The Abbot believed only Catholics should receive the holy Eucharist and chastised Nouwen, ordering him to give the host only to Catholics. Nouwen obeyed the abbot although he definitely did not agree with him.

My second favourite Nouwen book is *The Return of the Prodigal Son*, a meditation on Rembrandt's famous painting of Christ's parable. Nouwen so much loved the painting that he received permission to view it at the Hermitage Museum in Russia. For hours, he sat alone – an extraordinary permission on the part of the Soviet government – in front of the painting that had so moved and inspired him. The painting haunted him because it reminded him of his long-strained relationship with his father. Nouwen believed he was a failure in his father's eyes. Only when he was confined in the hospital recuperating after a near-fatal hit by a truck, did father and son resolve their differences – his father at the side of Nouwen's hospital bed.

Let us look again more closely at the prodigal son parable, where the son says, 'Father, give me the share of your estate that should come to me' (Luke 15:12). The impatient son refuses to wait for his father's natural death; in fact, he has a 'death wish' for his father in order to possess his inheritance now. In effect, the son is involved in psychological patricide, albeit unconsciously.

The father bestows upon his son his portion of his inheritance, and the young son willingly and gladly departs to a distant country where his life degenerates into one wildly prolonged, debauched party. We can imagine him with his many exploitative, fair-weather friends, squandering his inheritance on lust, wine and song. But soon the money vanishes and so do his friends, and he ends up alone and penniless. He hires himself out to local citizens who offer him a job tending the swine.

What a precipitous fall for this young man: to find himself working in a pigsty. To the Jewish people, pigs are symbols of impurity; therefore, in his culture, his occupation is the ultimate degradation. Having abandoned his father's house of love, he now feeds pigs, better fed and treated than he. Hunger for food reminds him of his father's house where the hired workers have more than enough to eat. Physical hunger also reminds him of his spiritual hunger: he desperately needs to be in the presence of human love, and decides to return home. At first, his decision to return home is the result not so much of sorrow but of pragmatism: he is poor and homeless. He also realises that he will have to exhibit contrition when he meets his father. He prepares a brief speech, 'Father, I have sinned against heaven and against you. I no longer deserve to be called your son; treat me as you would treat one of your hired workers' (Luke 15:18).

Is he really sorry for his actions? Has he admitted to himself his selfishness and egotism? Has he finally recognised his death wish for his father? We want to give him the benefit of the doubt and believe that he is full of remorse for laying waste his life and for being unloving towards his father, but we have to admit that it looks as if he is just weary of homelessness with its concomitant loneliness and hunger.

When the father sees his son in the distance, he is filled with compassion and eagerly runs towards him and embraces and repeatedly kisses him. Surely he smelled the odour of pigs on his son; he likely tasted on his son's lips the sweat, dust and grime of his son's former life. To his delight, his five senses dismiss the negatives, and he joyfully proclaims the return of his lost son, a return that is to him nearly incredible. His son who was 'dead' is alive again.

We have a parable macrocosmic in scope: it can be viewed as a narrative of humankind's journey from the time of Adam to now, or we can see it as a microcosmic story of a young man, a member of the human family, one who reeks of sin. The father's vision, however, penetrates beyond the filthy clothes, the odorous smells and degradation, all of which symbolise his son's sinful life. The eye of love sees through the foul surface to his son's true Self, and he immediately orders his servants to 'Quickly bring the finest robe and put it on him; put a ring on his finger and sandals on his feet' (Luke 15:22).

We have now before us an instant make-over. The external man is bathed, perfumed, newly attired, sandalled and bejewelled. The father reminds his son of his beloved son-ship. The father is not involved in a restoration of his son's status as a son, for in his mind and heart his son was never anything but his son; therefore, restoration is unnecessary.

We understand from a human standpoint that his father could have said, 'I told you so.' He could have said, 'Out of my sight! You are no longer worthy to be called my son.' He could have spoken something similar to literature's most powerful rejection of a child, King Lear's rejection of his daughter Cordelia:

> Here I disclaim all my paternal care,
> Propinquity, and property of blood,
> And as a stranger to my heart and me
> Hold thee from this forever.

Instead, the father orders what rightfully belongs to his son, commanding his servants to dress him in the 'finest robe'. Another translation says the 'best robe', but the Greek actually means the 'first robe'. Anthony Bloom suggests that he likely meant for his servants to retrieve the robe that his son had worn on the day he left, the one his son quickly tore off and carelessly discarded, the robe his father lovingly picked up, folded and put away as Isaac had done with his son Joseph's many-coloured robe spattered with the blood of his seeming death.

The father also offers his son a ring, which is not an ordinary ring. When people could not write, the ring was used as a seal to guarantee documents. To give one's ring to someone meant that you were placing your life into his or her hands.

The father asks nothing of his son; he wants only to have him back home where he can express his love for him, where he can relish his presence. And as in all cultures, the way to let people know you love and appreciate them is to throw a party. The father glee-fully shouts out the command, 'Take the fattened calf and slaughter it. Then let us celebrate with a feast, because this son of mine was dead, and has come to life again, he was lost and has been found' (Luke 15:24).

We can imagine the father's tacit plea, 'Let me love and treasure you because you are my beloved son. Let me celebrate your return. Let me proclaim to our world your value to me: you are more valuable than all my property, far beyond the worldly value of clothes, rings, and livestock.'

The father is, of course, offering his son a new life, a new innocence, a new start. The slate has been wiped clean. And because of the nature of agape – unconditional love – even if the son again falters and fails, he will be forgiven over and over again.

During his six-month stay at the Trappist Genesee Abbey in New York, Nouwen recorded in his diary a talk delivered by a visiting priest from St Bernard's Seminary in Rochester. The priest said that to convince someone of the beauty of the 12 stained-glass windows created by Marc Chagall for the synagogue of the Hadassah Hospital in Jerusalem, one had to show the windows from inside the synagogue. Nouwen was haunted by the idea that beauty could lure people into a gathering place for God-seekers.

From youth, Nouwen possessed an acute aesthetic sensibility, likely inherited from his parents, who, in fact, owned a Chagall painting, purchased before the artist achieved fame. His writings evidenced a love of literary expression. He admired the work of his fellow Dutch countryman Vincent van Gogh. Indeed, paintings especially seemed to imprint themselves upon Nouwen's mind and soul. In one of his most popular books, *Behold the Beauty of the Lord: Praying with Icons*, published in 1987, Nouwen offered meditations on four famous Russian paintings: the icon of the Holy Trinity (by Andrew Rublev, *c.* 1425), the icon of the Virgin of Vladimir (by an anonymous twelfth-century Greek), the icon of the Saviour of Zvenigorod (by Rublev), and the icon of the Descent of the Holy Spirit (fifteenth century, in the manner of the Novgorod School).

These icons inspired Nouwen to pray. At first, he fixed his attention upon the image. Because the images are beautiful, Nouwen needed no prodding to pay attention. He absorbed their beauty and artistry. The images then gradually spoke to his heart. Initially, the experience was aesthetic, but he then realised the source of the icons' beauty: God. Nouwen writes: 'an icon is like a window looking out upon eternity'.

Notice the journey: first, there is an image to focus upon; second, the image speaks to the viewer; third, the image leads to meditation, as gazing upon the image becomes prayer. In the next stage, still beyond Nouwen's reach, meditation will inexplicably move into contemplation – imageless prayer.

Contemplation is the form of prayer that many people find most difficult – not only to understand but also to practise. Most Christians prefer verbal prayer: reading the psalms, reciting the rosary, saying the Our Father, and other prayers of the Mass. Meditation entails thinking and visualisation, and many people approach it with a phrase from a prayer book or the Bible. The intellect cannot help in contemplation, however; in fact, during contemplation, the intellect is temporarily absent. Contemplation is nearly ineffable, but the personal encounters recalled by Nouwen surrounding Rembrandt's painting *The Return of the Prodigal Son* will help shed light on the experience of contemplation. Furthermore, if there is a painting in our world that best illustrates Jung's theory of individuation, it is Rembrandt's *Prodigal Son*.

The story of Nouwen and Rembrandt begins in 1983, when Nouwen was visiting L'Arche, a community for the handicapped, in Trosly, France (founded by Jean Vanier).

While conversing with a friend, Nouwen's gaze happened to fall upon a large poster of Rembrandt's *The Return of the Prodigal Son*. At the time, Nouwen had just returned from a gruelling six-week lecture tour through the United States. He writes:

> My heart leapt when I saw it. After my long self-exposing journey, the tender embrace of father and son expressed everything I desired at the moment. I was, indeed, the son exhausted from long travels; I wanted to be embraced. I was looking for a home where I could feel safe. The son-come-home was all I was and all that I wanted to be. For so long I had been going from place to place confronting, beseeching, admonishing, and consoling. Now I desired only to rest safely in a place where I could feel a sense of belonging, a place where I could feel at home.

One cannot find a more beautiful 'home' than Rembrandt's *c.* 1668 creation: its admixture of light and shadow, with shadow more abundant than light, is inviting, and draws the viewer into the narrative and its mystery. Nouwen was hooked, calling to mind Simone Weil's assertion that beauty is God's snare to lure us to him. Nouwen writes of the moment, 'I kept staring at the poster and finally stuttered (to his friend) "Its beautiful, more than beautiful … it makes me want to cry and laugh at the same time … I can't tell you what I feel as I look at it, but it touches me deeply." '

Nouwen did not realise at the time how profoundly this painting would change his life. After a
while, having only the poster proved insufficient to
him; he had to see for himself the original painting,
housed in the Hermitage Museum in Russia. So he
travelled to St Petersburg.

What did Nouwen behold there in Rembrandt's
shadows? We can never know (consider Jung's
theory of the archetypal shadow). What we do know
is that the painting before which he sat opened him
to the mystery of his life and more importantly to the
sublimity of God's love and compassion.

Let us consider Nouwen's account of the experience. He is in a room at the Hermitage; he is sitting in
a chair, gazing upon Rembrandt's painting. He
writes:

> As evening drew near, the sunlight grew more
> crisp and tingling. The embrace of the father
> and son became stronger and deeper, and the
> bystanders (in the painting) participated more
> directly in this mysterious event of reconcilia-
> tion, forgiveness and inner healing. Gradually
> I realized that there were as many paintings of
> the Prodigal Son as there were changes in the
> light, and, for a long time I was held spell-
> bound by the gracious dance of nature and art.

Then all of a sudden he writes, 'without my realizing
it, more than two hours had gone by when Alexi (the
guard) reappeared'. The contemplative experience is
a timeless moment. William James in his *The Varieties
of Religious Experience*, published in 1902, offers four
characteristics of the mystical experience: ineffabil-
ity, a 'noetic quality' (that is, a certain state of knowledge), transiency, and passivity. These apply as well

to the contemplative experience. For the contemplative, time flies. Or rather, it comes to a stop.

To be lost in beauty, in the beauty created by a man inspired by Christ's parable was a transcendent experience for Nouwen. He was with God Alone, not in any geographical place, but within his soul where God abides, at what Merton (borrowing from a student of Islam, Louis Massignon, who borrowed it from the Sufis) called the *point vierge* (virgin point). Merton writes in *Conjectures of a Guilty Bystander* (1966), 'At the centre of our being is a point of nothingness which is untouched by sin and by illusion, a point of pure truth, a point or spark which belongs entirely to God … This little point … is the pure glory of God in us.'

Let us now address the painting in Jungian terms. If you can, try to have a copy of the painting before you. Notice how much darkness there is in the painting. Many of the figures lurk in the shadows. One must look hard in order to see the woman in the upper left hand corner and the woman in the middle of the painting behind the father. Rembrandt was famous for using so much darkness in his paintings. From a Jungian perspective, this painting illustrates how so much of ourselves is buried in darkness, in the archetypal shadow of the unconscious mind. But if we look closely, we will see things that on a first look, we may miss. Is it not similar to individuation, which encourages us to gaze into our souls, to seek self-knowledge? At first glance, we would not know that the painting is not only of men. There are four men who dominate the painting; the father, the prodigal son, the elder son and another man (unidentified). But there are indeed women in the painting; in Jungian terms, they represent the archetypal anima. A painting of all men would be an imbalanced painting just as the life of a man without healthy relationships with women would be imbalanced and likely neurotic.

Notice the prodigal son. He is wearing rags for clothes. These rags were once fine clothes, but in his subsequent poverty, the result of wasting his inheritance on food, wine and lust, they now are torn and tattered, symbolic of his fragmented inner self. He is not a whole person. But he has finally turned his gaze from his egotistical way of life by shifting his gaze to Love: the love of his father, which is an unconditional love. Thus, we have a son, now stripped of all masks: he kneels before his father in humility. He is thoroughly himself. And his father accepts and loves him *as he is*: filthy, smelling of pigs, and likely flea-infested. His father lovingly embraces him.

Rembrandt is the master of shadow, but he is also the master of light. Notice where most of the painting's light is cast: on the father and the son. Rembrandt wants our gaze to focus on these two figures, for it is the lesson behind this that the artist wants to convey. The painting is one of Rembrandt's last. He is a broken man. He lost all his money, his fame, his family, and his beloved son Titus. He is alone in the world. And here before us, in his painting, is contained his final message, the message of Christ, 'Love, forgive and accept one another. It's all that matters.'

The shadow, the anima, the persona: all these archetypal aspects come together in a painting of utter beauty, a painting that I have not yet begun to fathom. A painting that Nouwen knew possessed a great secret, one he tried to solve, but he too in the end had to cease speaking about. There are indeed things in life that are ineffable.

Notes

1   Henri Nouwen, *The Road to Daybreak* (London: Darton, Longman & Todd, 1989), p. 223.
2   Henri Nouwen, *The Inner Voice of Love* (London: Darton, Longman & Todd, 1997), p. xv.
3   Ibid., p. xv.
4   Ibid., p. 116.

Questions for reflection

- Nouwen believed that we all need to recognise and accept our wounds. Have I done so?
- Depression is a psychic/spiritual wound. Have I learned to accept this fact about myself?
- Much of Nouwen's depressions related to his poor relationship with his father. Do I have unresolved conflicts with either or both of my parents?
- Nouwen for many years searched for a home, a place where he could be himself. Do I appreciate my home?
- When I am depressed, do I try my best not to allow depression to depress the members of my family, thus turning our home into an unhappy place?

- Nouwen never failed to turn to Christ in time of need. Do I realise that my greatest source of strength when depression hits is my Lord Jesus?
- When Nouwen had a nervous breakdown, he heeded the advice of friends to seek professional counsel. Do I listen to my family and friends? When they mention professional assistance, do I dismiss them, or do I take their concern seriously.

7

Philip Toynbee: A Depressive in Search of Meaning

Philip Toynbee is the son of the eminent historian Arnold Toynbee. His grandfather was the famous classicist Gilbert Murray. Thus, we can safely say that Toynbee comes from a rather distinguished English family, of which he was rightfully proud. He himself became one of the *Observer's* most distinguished book reviewers, an occupation he took very seriously, winning the respect of many writers of many genres.

He was also a poet and a diarist. Toynbee wrote two spiritual diaries: *Part of a Journey, An Autobiographical Journal 1977–1979* and *End of a Journey 1979–1981*. Toynbee will be remembered for these two remarkable journals because he is brutally honest about himself, baring his soul. He was a well known agnostic, drinker, and anti-Christian, particularly anti-Catholic after his mother converted to Catholicism, an act he had at first viewed as both a familial and social betrayal. Yet in 1963, in a published dialogue with his grandfather, Toynbee says, 'I suppose the most fundamental question anyone could ask anyone else is, do you believe in God?' This posed question initiated the first tentative steps of his spiritual quest. By the time he wrote his first journal, Toynbee had recovered his belief in God, a beleaguered faith, but faith nevertheless.

His journals are fraught with doubt, fear, and crippling depression (self-medicated by alcohol and prescribed pills), to be gradually followed by periods of clarity, epiphany and joy. Above his sometimes calm, sometimes chaotic life hovers the presence of the spiritual master whom Toynbee most admired, Thomas Merton. That he found a kindred spirit in Merton is not surprising, for they had much in common: both had mothers stinting in their display of love and affection. Both were born writers, with a poetic sensibility. Both were intellectuals educated at English grammar schools and universities. Both were acutely aware of the social injustices of contemporary life. Both flirted with the Communist Party. Both were agnostics in their youth. Both were inveterate readers. Both were healthy heterosexuals with an eye for attractive women. Both read and admired the French mystic Simone Weil. Both chose Dame Julian of Norwich as their favourite mystic.

What Toynbee found in Merton was utter honesty about the spiritual life. He also admired Merton as a gifted writer but above all he respected his concern for his fellow brothers and sisters.

Toynbee did not live long enough to have had the privilege of reading either Merton's unexpurgated journals or his collected letters, but his early opinion of Merton holds up extremely well as an insightful summary of what Merton had become by the end of his life, and Toynbee understood the importance of the role Merton played in the realm of spirituality in the latter part of the twentieth century, and possessed the clarity of sight to know that in Merton he had found what in theological terms we call a *proficient*, someone who knows the mystical journey to God because he has travelled it.

In many ways Toynbee was a selfish man. His ego was huge, and he was an annoying drunk, hurting people by saying outrageous things and simply being obnoxious, about which he frankly (and contritely) writes in his journal. He had yet to learn that the secret of individuation is to shift attention away from the ego. But on November 12, 1977, Toynbee writes an astounding journal entry in which he describes stopping by a tree on his property and just gazing at it. He experienced not only a deep appreciation for its beauty but also a deep melancholy, one that felt the 'tears at the heart of things'. Memories of his childhood arose from his unconscious, of a once innocent boy gazing upon trees and upon nature. So lifted from his self-consciousness, he often stopped before this tree and simply looked with such an intensity that he experienced a self-forgetting. He saw into the nature of things, observing the tree's singularity, its uniqueness, its right to be. It was one of a kind, and no other tree could ever take its place. His was a piercing insight because it is also applicable to every human being: each person is a one of a kind. This mystery penetrated him so deeply that he began to practice the art of attention, for if a tree can offer such insight, perhaps if he were attentive to other things in nature, he would be granted further 'seeings' or to use Dame Julian's expression, 'shewings.'

It is not unusual for an aspect of nature to remind one of God (God made all things). Think of Brother Lawrence, writer of the spiritual classic, *The Practice of the Presence of God*. His greatest mystical experience about God's power and presence occurred when he found himself gazing upon a tree. And consider how important the tree became in the history of Christianity, for the tree is the symbol of life and renewal, and it also, through Christ's crucifixion upon the cross, the symbol of our salvation; the tree of the cross is symbolically composed from the Tree of Knowledge

in the Garden of Eden. Through the cross sin and
death would be vanquished, its horizontal beam representing the world, its vertical beam the direct com-
munication with earth and heaven.

By the time Toynbee's journal was published, he
was ill and died two months after its publication (his
second journal was published posthumously). *Part of
a Journey* zeroes in on Toynbee's severe depression
and his emergence from it, primarily by his developing a spiritual life; in short, he turned to God. The
latter inspired him to aim for self-improvement, not
only as an individual, but also as a husband, father,
friend-and as a Christian.

The theme of Toynbee's first journal, he wrote, was
his search for God, and his thoughts and feelings
about his own emotional life, and depression gener-
ally, were woven through it. For example he writes
about his desire to convince his 'Depressive Anonymous friends' to gather to form groups to support
one another, recognizing at the same time that this
might be an impossibility.

His own experiences, he believes, can be used by
God 'for our own hallowing' to quote de Caussade.
The breaking apart of the world he had constructed
leads him to fall back on faith and hope, and a world
in which he had hitherto felt 'imprisoned' becomes
more like an open road.

For Toynbee, the beauty of Christ's message is that
he died to prevent the reduction of the world to dull
formula. His life and his message is constant renewal
in the Now moment: 'Behold I make all things new.'

The spiritual writers of this century who speak to
him most directly are Thomas Merton and Simone
Weil, and he reflects on the contrast: Merton is in the
traditional mould, wise, unhurried, and grounded in

tradition; Weil is a sparkling intellect, searching, grabbing and hungry for truth.

He finds thrilling and enlivening De Caussade's timeless message to live every moment of our lives as if it were our last. He strives to live in the Now, but is dragged down with memories. He wishes he could walk freely without their terrible weight. And yet, he admits, those memories possess their own value, for without them he would never have embarked on the journey to God, never have known that it is in self-forgetting that we find God.

He asserts that he is a Christian because of the Christ, a man able to pierce our ego-laden self, and he believes in the power of prayer; believes that when he says, 'Lord, the Light of the World, have mercy on me and shed your Light upon my poor self, one lost, afraid, and blind' that prayer is heard. The man who sacrificed his life for the world, knows and loves his unique self.

The concept of God as judge, Toynbee points out, has done much harm to humankind: an idea springing from the belief that God knows our hidden selves. To know all is to forgive all, however, for in God, as Dame Julian reminds us, there is No blame.

Toynbee contrasts his existence as an ordinary man – a heap of pride, ambition, anxieties, all blocking divine light – with another part of the self which is a vehicle for God's love and illumination. He writes of a vain search for the divine spark within, finding that the more he searches, the more he realizes that it is God's light seeking his own light; that the divine light is One and we are all a part of it.

In the world he finds it is difficult to hold onto hope, but Toybee finds solace in many different places: the words of Dame Julian's promise from Christ, 'All shall be well'; in Jesus the Light of the

World, where he finds a piercing icon of uplifiting words; and in God's agapetic love in which he finds his reason for being.

Christ's prayer, 'Thy Will be Done' he finds challenging to his ego, while asking for forgiveness is easier.

As we can see, the journal gives us a brief but illuminating view of Toynbee's inner landscape. He would be the first to tell us that it was not a pretty sight. He knew it, and took upon himself the role of self-gardener. He understood that there were many weeds of bad habits and thinking that needed pruning or uprooting. He knew also that his inner garden demanded watering and reseeding. And he took his job seriously. He wanted indeed to see new growth, green grass, flowering trees, and flowing water. And he accomplished a rebirth of his soul: although he would certainly not say that 'he' did it himself. He would likely say that God opened his eyes to what is important in life, and that he finally paid attention.

The reason why I began this chapter on Toynbee with his exquisite seeing of a tree is that I believe that Toynbee had been blind to so much about life and about himself. Blind in the sense that his gaze was not allowed to shift from his ego to anything Other. What he paid more attention to than anything else in life was his reading of books and his reviewing of them. He greatly neglected his wife and his family. When they needed his attention, his eyes were more likely reading or involved in writing a review. He also spent much of his time writing verse, poetry he was unable to have published, so it is impossible for us to know if he was a competent/gifted poet or not (some of his poetry is included in his second journal, *End of Journey*).

As he stated himself, the two religious writers he read and admired most were Simone Weil and Thomas Merton. I am convinced that Toynbee took to heart Weil's famous and controversial definition of prayer, 'Absolutely unmixed attention is prayer.' When I later realized how much he admired her, I knew that Philip Toynbee and I were kindred spirits: we were also in agreement about Thomas Merton, whom I believe Toynbee not only admired, but loved. And he nearly admired Weil as much as he did Merton. He does not reveal in his journal much knowledge about the biography of Weil, more about what she wrote. I think he would have identified with her had he known that she too suffered from depression and terrible migraines. She did not turn to alcohol, a form of self-punishment, but to an equally egregious self-inflicted 'penance': denying herself sufficient and healthy food. She was a classic sufferer of anorexia nervosa, a disease whose origin is psychological, linked to depression and low self-esteem, sometimes self-loathing. She died by refusing to eat in a hospital in Kent, her doctor being Dr Tom Bennett, who had been Thomas Merton's guardian after his father died.

I believe we can understand Toynbee better by knowing more about Simone Weil. So the following excerpts from my own journal, I believe, will shed light on both Toynbee and Weil:

The following is an excerpt from the author's private journal.

When I first read the work of Simone Weil, I felt as if a new world of the spirit had been opened to me, as had happened years ago when I had first read Thomas Merton. One of her epigrammatic sentences took my breath away: 'Absolutely unmixed attention is prayer'.

Over the years I had read many books about 'how to pray,' and for a time I followed their methodology about centering prayer, repeating mantras, breathing deeply, employing various mudras (postures), warding off unwanted thoughts, and practicing more complicated ways of praying, like the Ignatian method of composition of place; however, I rarely felt spiritually nourished, my focus painstakingly fixed on the methodology of posture, mantra, breath and imagination than actual prayer; thus, my jumbled efforts invariably dissolved into frustration and inattention.

Weil's definition of prayer, however, stunned me. I looked up the meaning of *attention*: 'Concentration of the mental powers upon an object; a close or careful observing or listening.' Nothing complicated here. We are all capable of concentration, close observation and listening; therefore, according to Weil, we all should be capable of prayer.

Like Thomas Merton, she advocates no system of prayer. She simply states that prayer is losing ourselves in an act of attention: it alone opens us to the Divine, illustrating the Biblical counsel: 'In losing yourself you will find yourself.' To pay attention, however, necessitates a self-forgetting, a surrendering of ourselves to the object of our attention. Weil writes:

> Attention consists of suspending our thought, leaving it detached, empty and ready to be penetrated by the object. It means holding in our minds, within reach of this thought, but on a lower level and not in contact with it, the diverse knowledge we have acquired which we are forced to make use of ... Above all, our thought should be empty, waiting, not seeking anything, but ready to receive in its naked truth the object which is to penetrate it.[1] (*The Simone Weil Reader*, edited by George A. Panichas, New York: David McKay Company, Inc., 1977, p. 49.)

Weil's definition of *attention* correlates with Thomas Merton's definition of contemplation:

> Contemplation is the highest expression of man's intellectual and spiritual life. It is that life itself, fully awake, fully active, fully aware that it is alive. It is spiritual wonder. (Thomas Merton, *New Seeds of Contemplation*, New York: New Directions Press, 1961, p. 1.)

'Fully awake', 'fully active', 'fully aware': it all sounds like an excellent description of Weil's concept of *attention*, a state of being akin to wonder. I am reminded of Christ's dictum that unless we are as children, we shall not enter the kingdom of heaven. It almost goes without saying that children possess a sense of wonder; thus, to enter God's Kingdom, we must somehow retrieve our sense of wonder, accomplished, I am now convinced, by developing our powers of attention.

I will never forget my discovery of Weil's essay, 'Reflections on the Right Use of School Studies.' As a teacher, the title naturally caught my attention, and it transformed my way of thinking about education, causing me to change my teaching methods. She writes:

> If we concentrate our attention on trying to solve a problem of geometry, and if at the end of an hour we are no nearer to doing so than at the beginning, we have nevertheless been making progress each minute of that hour in another more mysterious dimension. Without our knowing or feeling it, this apparently barren effort has brought more light into the soul. The result will one day be discovered in prayer. (*The Simone Weil Reader*, p. 45)

She states that every act of attention prepares us for contact with divinity. Learning, she believes, can only happen when one forgets oneself. To become selfless requires putting the ego on the back burner of the mind. In that moment of egolessness, the mind and soul can then be penetrated by the Other. Prayer is similar: if there is to be contact with God in prayer, one must forget oneself totally. Thus, education with its emphasis on attention, Weil insists, is a preparation for prayer. To my mind, her theory is *revolutionary*. I was gratified to think that during my many years of teaching I had actually been preparing my students for the possibility of a spiritual life.

Weil was French by birth, Jewish by heritage. She was attracted to Catholicism, but never was baptized into the church. As a student she won top academic honours, but at first her great empathy for the poor led her not to the academy but to work in factories where she became friends with working people. She also fought in the Spanish Civil War and later devoted her service to the Free French movement. She lived her life according to strict moral standards, and when she was ill in an English hospital, she would not eat anything more than what the French were permitted to eat in rations. Some say she died of starvation. Today she is famous as a French writer and mystic, and to some she is a martyr.

Two of her mystical experiences are worth mentioning. The first involves Weil's meeting an Englishman at the monastery of Solesmes, famous for its Gregorian chant. In 1938, Weil and her mother were spending ten days at Solesmes, from Palm Sunday to Easter Tuesday. At the abbey Weil met a young English Catholic who recommended that she read the English poets of the seventeenth century. She read George Herbert's 'Love,' a poem that so tremendously moved her, she memorized it and often recited it aloud. It was during a recitation, she says, that 'Christ himself came down and took possession of me'.

At Solesmes, she suffered from terrible migraines; any sound pounded her like blows to the head, but she found release in the 'unimaginable beauty of the chanting of the words.' Her experience of Gregorian chant may not have been a mystical one, but it was certainly a numinous one.

At another time, she was visiting Assisi. Alone in the little twelfth-century church of Santa Maria degli Angeli where St Francis prayed, she felt the presence and purity of St Francis. She writes, 'something stronger than I compelled me for the first time in my life to go down on my knees.'

Philip Toynbee and Simone Weil, two twentieth-century intellectuals in search of meaning, in search of God. And the search was successful.

Bibliography

Philip Toynbee, *Part of a Journey*, *An Autobiographical Journal 1977–1979* (London: Collins 1981).

J.C. Cooper *An Illustrated Encyclopaedia of Traditional Symbols* (London: Thames and Hudson, 1978), p. 178.

George A. Panichas, *The Simone Weil Reader*, (New York: The McKay Company, Inc. 1977).

Questions to ask oneself

- Do I rely on alcohol as a means to self-medicate during my depression?
- If I do drink too much, have I sought counselling?
- What has Toynbee taught me about the spiritual journey?
- Like Toynbee, do I have an outlet, like journaling, writing poetry, or reading that will assuage the symptoms of depression?
- Do I find myself neglecting my family during my depression and what steps can I take to rectify it?
- Can I deal with my depression on my own, or do I need professional counsel?

8

Thomas Merton's Integration of the Shadow and Anima

Thomas Merton suffered from depression. In his autobiography, *The Seven Storey Mountain* (as well as in his journals), he records many instances of his depression. On at least two occasions he was tempted to commit suicide.

He lost his mother to cancer when he was six years old, and when he was about to turn sixteen, he lost his father, again to cancer. He was very close to his father, and his death had a profound effect on the teenager. Let us look at Merton sitting in a room alone while his father was dying in a London hospital. He writes:

> I sat there in the dark, unhappy room, unable to think, unable to move, with all the innumerable elements of my isolation crowding in upon me from every side: without a home, without a family, without a country, without a father, apparently without any friends, without interior peace or confidence or light or understanding of my own – without God, too, without God, without heaven, without grace, without anything.[1]

Merton again negatively describes his 16-year-old self: 'I now belonged to the world in which I lived. I became a true citizen of my disgusting century.'[2] On returning from a walking tour of Germany to his prep school, Oakham, he writes: 'But I now lay on this bed, full of gangrene, and my soul was rotten with the corruption of my sins. And I did not even care whether I died or lived.'[3]

All of the above youthful descriptions are heart-rending. So young and so unhappy! We feel great sympathy for this young man who feels so abandoned. To this reader, the saddest part of his self-evaluation is his realisation that he is homeless and Godless. Thus, as a young adult the major search for Merton will be to find a home and to find God. Without either, he would indeed become one of T. S. Eliot's 'hollow men', living a life of quiet desperation.

After his father's death, Merton goes off the rails. He embarks upon a reckless life, pursuing pleasure in various forms. As a teenager, he fathers a child, and at this point his guardian Tom Bennett, a friend of Merton's father, cuts the cord of responsibility by advising Merton to remain in America and begin a new life. Merton obeys his guardian's counsel and transfers from Cambridge University to Columbia University in New York City. However, in his autobiography he delivers one last shot at Cambridge, England:

> I am even willing to admit that some people might live there for three years, or even a lifetime, so protected that they never sense the sweet stench of corruption that is all around them – the keen, thin scent of decay that pervades everything ... the bitter taste is still with me after not a few years.[4]

This seems to be quite unfair to Cambridge. With its beautiful quads, its flowing Cam and King's Chapel with its exquisite fan vaulting, Cambridge has some of the most beautiful colleges in the world, but to Merton it was hell on earth. Why? His commentary is an example of psychological projection. Cambridge is not filled with corruption and decay, but it is to Thomas Merton. He has to face the fact that he has not been living an exemplary life. And until he recognises this fact and does something about it, he will remain the depressed, unhappy young man he has become.

His search is not a long one. By converting, he finds a home in the Catholic Church. And then he chooses a place to live: the Abbey of Gethsemani in Kentucky where he wins some peace as a Trappist monk and priest. But even in the abbey, *c.* 1957, 16 years after entering the Trappist order, he still suffered from bouts of depression. We see it in the following poem:

Whether There Is Enjoyment in Bitterness

> This afternoon, let me
> Be a sad person. Am I not
> Permitted (like other men)
> To be sick of myself?
>
> Am I not allowed to be hollow,
> Or fall in the hole
> Or break my bones (within me)
> In the trap set by my own
> Lie to myself? O my friend,
> I too must sin and sin.
>
> I too must hurt other people and
> (Since I am no exception)
> I must be hated by them.

Do not forbid me, therefore
To taste the same bitter poison.
And drink the gall that love
(Love most of all) so easily becomes.

Do not forbid me (once again) to be
Angry, bitter, disillusioned
Wishing I could die.

While life and death
Are killing one another in my flesh,
Leave me in peace. I can enjoy,
Even as other men, this agony.

Only (whoever you may be)
Pray for my soul. Speak my name
To Him, for in my bitterness
I hardly speak to Him: and He
While He is busy killing me
Refuses to listen.

Notice in the above poem the words: 'hollow', 'poison', 'gall', 'angry', 'disillusioned', 'bitterness' and 'agony'. They suggest a man in spiritual and psychological pain and turmoil. The last stanza is an echo from one of Gerard Manley Hopkins' 'terrible sonnets'; in fact, it is the same complaint Hopkins made (Merton had greatly admired Hopkins, and at Columbia had intended to write his dissertation on him). Hopkins writes:

But ah, but O thou terrible, why wouldst thou rude
    on me
The wring-world right foot rock? Lay lionlimb
    against me?

Why, Hopkins asks, is God, as strong as a lion, pun-ishing him, exerting his great 'lionlimb' strength against him. And later, in another terrible sonnet, Hopkins laments that God does not listen to him, 'And my lament/Is cries countless, cries like dead letters sent/To dearest him that lives alas! away.' God is deaf to him.

Merton, like all of us, had his bad days. It is part of the human condition, one Merton fully understood, having dealt with severe depression when he was a young man. There was also the day in a hotel room when he was a youth: the window beckoned him to kill himself by jumping from it. Indeed, there was another temptation to suicide while riding a Man-hattan train, an inner voice enticed him to throw himself from the train to the tracks below him.

Well acquainted with the dark night of the soul, Merton, as an adult, survived by writing and turning to poetry – Dante, Blake, Hopkins and Eliot were his spiritual mentors – inspired him to live. A monk, Merton's daily celebration of the Mass and his pray-ing of the lectio divina were also supports in his battle against depression, for, as Jung repeatedly comments, every patient he had observed cured had regained a spiritual perspective on life.

In late 1957, Merton was still trying to understand his young self. He writes in his journal of the guilt and resentment he feels about moving to America: claiming to despise European bourgois values; at the same time he also disparages his grandfather's faith in America and what it stands for. Where does this leave him, he wonders, recognising that the dilemma is an important part of his life, and is one which he must explore and understand.

Merton is again involved in psychological projec-tion. This time he is projecting his 'guilt' and 'resent-

ment' upon larger entities, America and Europe, but
the fault lies, as Shakespeare reminds us, not in the
stars (or anything, for that matter) but in ourselves.
He seemingly resents his grandfather's optimism.
Why? Because at the time he had turned into a pessimist, who believed the world was going to hell in a
hand basket, the bad fruit of his own *contemptus
mundi* (contempt of the world). It is quite easy to see
the splinter in another's eye but not the beam in
one's own. His use of the word 'hollower' is again an
echo of T. S. Eliot's poem 'The Hollow Men', a poem
Merton knew well, having long been an admirer of
Eliot. And he likely agreed with Eliot's take on the
modern world: the modern world was a wasteland.
Merton escaped it by converting to Catholicism and
entering a contemplative order. Eliot escaped it by
converting to the Church of England and by living a
pious life of daily Mass and prayer.

Both men felt, and were wise in their decision, that
the cure for their spiritual and psychological malaise
lay in religion, and neither ever doubted that they
had done the right thing by embracing Christianity.
If both men had not found God, they may have
indeed taken their lives, for both had flirted with
self-slaughter.

In 1957, Merton went to the hospital for an operation. He wrote that this experience unleashed 'subconscious terror' in him. Poor health can cause
depression. Being in a hospital underscores our
physical vulnerability; it also reminds us of our mor-
tality. Merton had always believed that he would die
young, a fear that proved to be true. But his sense of
'despair' makes one take pause because, again, one
would like to believe that a man who is a priest
would not be a victim to despair. We want to believe
that God offers his priests the grace to avoid such a

serious and debilitating spiritual illness. But priests are human; thus, they are subject to the same suffering to which any other human being is prone. In that sense, we are all in the same boat.

Notice the phrase 'subconscious terror'. It proves that Merton had no doubt about Freud and Jung's belief in the subconscious. It also shows us that he understands that the subconscious is the very locus into which we repress what frightens us. So we ask: what terrified Merton? Surely death is a possibility. Even if one believes in God and the immortality of the soul, such belief does not nullify one's fear of death. In fact, it may enhance one's fear because a Christian knows that at death there is to be a judgement, and many Christians, particularly Catholics, fear God's judgement, having been raised with an image of God founded not so much on Love but on Justice. And if any of us were to be gifted with a choice between the two, Love or Justice, we would surely choose Love, for who among us could pass the test of Justice?

Merton's poem and journals reveal a struggling man. Too many of Merton's readers want to believe that once Merton had entered the Abbey of Gethsemani, his life was a serene one of peace and contemplation. Well, the fact of the matter is that entrance into the abbey was only the beginning of Merton's inner journey. And over the years as a dedicated monk, he, indeed, learned that his doubts, fears, anger, sadness, depressions, guilt and resentment are all part of his life, and he accepts them – we know this because in his journals he makes no effort to hide these aspects of himself from his readers but shares them.

From a Jungian perspective, it is obvious that Merton is still trying to understand the shadow aspects of his personality (through writing about them), but depression can still rear its ugly head when least expected. The advantage that Merton has is that he can transmute his pain and suffering into art: into poetry and into the lucid, beautiful prose of his journals. When Merton's unexpurgated journals were published, we learned the degree to which Merton had been influenced by Jung. In his entry of 11 August 1962, Merton quotes Jung's assertion that people will do anything to avoid facing their own psyches. They will try anything to avoid this because they cannot 'get on with themselves', and do not believe anything useful could ever come from it.

His emphasis here reveals much about what Merton felt about the exploration of the psyche. He had been well trained by the Catholic Church to examine his conscience, but it was Jung (and Freud) who encouraged him to delve into his unconscious mind. It is no wonder then that he began to record his dreams; to employ Jung's words; he found them 'useful' because they 'come out of the psyche'.

We are not to assume that Merton was always depressed. His depressions came and went. Proof of this can be found in his ecstatic Louisville Vision, in which Merton finally casts aside his *contemptus mundi* and embraces the world in love. In Louisville he was overwhelmed by the realisation that he loved everyone and that every person belonged each to the other. He experienced 'the immense joy of being human'.

This is a pivotal moment in his individuation, for it shows us that Merton has accomplished much soul-work, that he is not projecting his shadow onto the world, that he has begun to integrate it; thus, he has removed the cataracts from his spiritual eyes and is able to see the beauty of God's people in the world.

He has learned to love his own shadow. Consider the following by James Hillman:

> Loving the shadow may begin with carrying it, but even that is not enough. At one moment something else must break through, that laughing insight at the paradox of one's own folly which is also everyman's. Then may come the joyful acceptance of the rejected and inferior, a going with it and even a partial living of it. This love may even lead to an identification with and acting-out of the shadow, falling into its fascination. Therefore the moral dimension can never be abandoned. Thus is a cure a paradox requiring two incommensurables: the moral recognition that these parts of me are burdensome and intolerable and must change, and the loving laughing acceptance which takes them just as they are, joyfully, forever. One both tries hard and lets go, both judges harshly and joins gladly. Western moralism and Eastern abandon: each holds only one side of the truth.[5]

When one reads the above, one cannot forget Merton's description of himself as a person living in the belly of a paradox (see his book, *The Sign of Jonas*).

It would be useful in our understanding of Merton to juxtapose one of our century's greatest spiritual masters with one of our century's greatest psychiatrists, who would likely describe himself as a 'doctor of souls'. Jung and Merton share so many things in common. Let us consider a few of them.

During Jung's mid-life crisis, he could never have faced the turmoil of his unconscious without the help of the feminine; in his case, it was his wife

Emma and his lover Antonia Wolff. It is not unusual
for a man to turn to an anima figure at mid-life, and
she is usually quite young. Toni Wolff was only 23
years old when Jung fell in love with her. The amaz-
ing thing is that his wife was so tolerant of the situa-
tion, but she loved her husband, and being a wise
woman herself about a man's individuation, she
allowed Wolff into their lives.

At mid-life Jung also reconnected with his religious traditions, abandoned when he was a disciple
of Freud. He again rediscovered his soul, which led
to his writing the ground-breaking book, *Modern
Man in Search of a Soul.* Jung became the hero of his
inner journey, and, like a young Parsifal, he searched
for the Holy Grail of psychic/spiritual wholeness:

> He had gone out into the world, had chal-
> lenged the leading knights (peers) of the scien-
> tific community and he learned the world and
> he had won his spurs. He had become a man.
> No longer the dumb young Parsifal was he. As
> a youth he had stood by feeling helpless
> watching his father die. He did not know what
> to say to his father, did not even know what to
> ask. Later he was to learn the significance of
> Parsifal's question 'Whom does the Grail
> serve?' and the answer 'It serves the Grail
> King.' He came to realize that the Grail King is
> the Self, that center of our interior castle, that
> circle whose center is everywhere and whose
> circumference is nowhere.[6]

Now let us look at Thomas Merton. Does not the
above description of Jung's helplessness describe
Merton's own description of himself in the London
hospital room with his father dying of cancer? Mer-

ton too is reduced to silence, not knowing what to say. His father had strewn across his bed drawings that looked like small holy icons. Merton never forgot this. Was his father trying to communicate to his son a newly found belief, a newly found faith in something beyond physical life?

Merton, like Jung, embarks upon life like a knight, like a young Parsifal. He must be, as must all of us, the hero of his life. He may not have to slay dragons, but he will have to slay certain fears, doubts, anxieties and phobias. He will have to seek the meaning of life, symbolised by the Holy Grail. For Jung most of his knight-pursuit is accomplished in the arena of psychology. For Merton it will be in the arena of spirituality. But who are to be his feminine supports, his anima figures? Because he chooses to become a priest, he cannot marry or have a lover. Mother Church will be his support and the Abbey of Gethsemani, dedicated to Mary the Mother of God.

For many years these two feminine forces (Mother Church and the Blessed Mother) help Merton to live his life. They help him to pass through the difficult times, through the fears and depression. They suffice; but in the end, they both prove to be not quite enough. He will need the support of a real woman. And when he had to be admitted to a Louisville hospital for an operation, he meets a young nurse in her twenties, and he falls in love with her, and she with him.

In Louisville, Merton had experienced a universal feeling of love, what Jung would describe as a 'participation mystique', when a person cannot distinguish himself from the object but is bound to it by a direct relationship which amounts to partial identification. But now he is in love, not with a collective but with an individual. She is his beloved, in whom he loses himself. Because of her, he becomes more alive, tingling with new life, new desires, new hopes, and new dreams.

Prior to meeting the nurse, Merton believed he had found the Holy Grail. The Holy Grail is the cup Christ used at the Last Supper; therefore it has come to symbolise Christ himself. For Merton, a dedicated priest and monk, Christ should be enough to render him a happy, whole human being. But there is the human factor: God can surely 'touch' a person, but people also need to be touched physically by another human being. As the poet Anne Sexton says, 'Touch is all.' The touch of a woman is the very kind of touch Merton had longed for all his life. Not the touch of lust: he knew well that kind of touch. What he had longed for, and denied himself by becoming a celibate priest and monk, was the touch of love. We know that Merton viewed his mother as a 'severe mother'. She was stinting in her expression of love. And she may be the cause of what he describes as his life-long 'refusal of woman'. Now, all of a sudden, a young woman is actually in love with him! And finally he is touched both spiritually and physically.

Jung and Merton, both in search of the Holy Grail. Jung found it with the help of two women, in the archetypal Self (the archetypal Christ). And Merton, with the help of Mother Church and Mary our Blessed Mother, found Christ within the walls of the Abbey of Gethsemani. But beyond the safety of its enclosing walls he found human love in the arms of a young woman. We cannot fault him for this, for it was part of his journey of individuation. To judge him would be to fail to obey Christ's dictum, 'Judge not lest ye be judged' (Luke 6:37). Keep in mind that Merton ended the affair, and he remained a priest and monk at Gethsemani.

Notes

1   Thomas Merton, *The Seven Storey Mountain* (New York: Harcourt Brace Co., 1948), p. 79.
2   Ibid., p. 85.
3   Ibid., p. 99.
4   Ibid., p. 39.
5   James Hillman, *Insearch: Psychology and Religion* (Woodstock: Spring Publications, 1994), pp. 76–7.
6   John-Raphael Staude, *The Adult Development of C. G. Jung* (London: Routledge & Kegan Paul, 1981), p. 38.

Questions for reflection

- Thomas Merton is one of the greatest spiritual masters of the twentieth century. Have I made myself familiar with his life by reading his auto-biography?
- Is my depression linked with the way I live? Am I doing anything in my life that demands that I seek a priest and absolution?
- Are my goals for myself realistic? Am I, like the young Merton, seeking an impossible goal like perfection or sainthood?
- Have I made prayer a part of my daily life?
- When was the last time I read the psalms? The monastic prayer life revolves around the psalms, poems that address every important aspect of life from birth to love to suffering to death.

- The motto over the entrance of the Abbey of Gethsemani is 'God Alone'. Do I realise that in my life also God must be my number-one consideration?
- Have I learned, as had Merton, that the spiritual life cannot begin unless one is able to forgive, and that forgiveness begins with forgiving oneself?

9

Loran Hurnscot: From Depression to Mystical Ecstasy

Thirty years ago I fell in love with a book, *A Prison, A Paradise* (Victor Gollancz, 1958), by Loran Hurnscot. A colleague of mine, who had lost a daughter to cancer, said this book had helped her live her last year, one fraught with pain and suffering, with peace and courage. When I expressed an interest in the book, he gave me his British version, keeping for himself his daughter's American copy. The book is a stunning diary. Volume One chronicles the author's doomed marriage and simultaneous love affair, the latter encouraged by her husband dying from consumption. It reminded me of the best of D. H. Lawrence's writing, not only for its frank treatment of human sexuality and love but also for its delicately lyrical descriptions of the English countryside, both its flora and weather. Volume Two begins after her husband had died, leaving her with a pittance of an annuity and causing her lover to abandon her. It charts her spiritual search, one that journeys into several different, unfulfilling philosophies until she succumbs to depression and despair, finally deciding to take her own life. One of the world's foremost Jungian therapists says about suicide:

> Under the pressure of 'too late', knowing that life went wrong and there is no longer a way out, suicide offers itself. Then suicide is the

urge for hasty transformation. This is not premature death, as medicine might say, but the late reactions of a delayed life which did not transform as it went along. It would die all at once, and now, because it missed its death crises before. This impatience and intolerance reflects a soul that did not keep pace with its life; or, in older people, a life that no longer nourishes with experiences a still-hungering soul.[1]

What Hurnscot truly wants is transformation, but she will not actively seek it until she experiences her flirtation with suicide. In a sense she has to 'get it (self-slaughter) out of her system'. She had long known of a river in Yorkshire, which narrowed to three feet or so, into which the suicidal threw themselves, only to be swept under into limestone caves never to be found again. She settled her personal affairs, disguised herself so as not to be recognised and travelled by train to the river. Poised upon the bank's rocks, she was prepared to end her life when the sheer evil of the place and the sorrowful presence of past suicides swept over her. Hurnscot writes:

> I cried hopelessly for a long while. I looked again at the water, and thought of the Dial in my bag, that I meant to swallow to deaden consciousness. A tremendous 'NO' rose – within me? Outside me? I don't know. 'I can't do it – I'm held back. I know beyond all doubt that it is absolutely wrong.'[2]

She finally concludes that it was God who prevented her death. She prays, 'I'm in Your hands … You stopped me. You must show me what to do.'[3] It was the earnest beginning of her spiritual journey.

I knew nothing about the true identity of Loran Hurnscot, her name a pseudonym. My research yielded nothing. The only clues I had to go on were those that the poet Kathleen Raine revealed in her Introduction to *A Prison, A Paradise* where she states that the author wished to remain unknown, for she lived her life according to the Taoist maxim, 'Keep your life hidden.' Raine also wrote about Hurnscot: 'There is no mistaking the authentic note that comes only from lived experience; she writes of the discovery of the divine life with the sureness of Teresa, Julian, and Guyon, and with a like humility.'[4]

While browsing in a used bookshop in Boston, I noticed a three-volume autobiography by Kathleen Raine. I had known Raine as one of the world's pre-eminent William Blake scholars; I was also aware that she was a highly respected poet (both T. S. Eliot and W. B. Yeats had read and admired her verse), although I had not yet sampled her verse (I now have and enjoy her spare, lucid lyrics). Holding her small, attractive autobiographical volumes in my hand, I decided to purchase them in the hope that she might drop a hint about the identity of Loran Hurnscot.

I vividly remember reading the second volume, *The Land Unknown* (pp. 87–91), when Raine refers to her dear friend Gay Taylor, aka Loran Hurnscot. My heart leapt: at last I knew her identity! Loran Hurnscot (an anagram of what she believed were her two besetting sins, sloth and rancour) was Gay Taylor, wife of Hal Taylor, the founder of England's famous Golden Cockerel Press, admired for publishing beautiful hand-printed books.

I contacted the eminent poet Raine; she welcomed any inquiry about Gay Taylor whom she considered a great, if not her greatest friend. She offered me information about Gay's husband and her lover (writer A. E. Coppard), as well as a portrait of Gay's life as a spiritual seeker. She said that although Gay never joined any church, since she considered herself one of God's goats, she often sought empty churches where she prayed in solitude. Gay was a great believer in intercessory prayer, and she would list on paper the names of those for whom she prayed. Kathleen Raine was very much touched to find upon Gay's death, her own name on the list of names. Like me, Raine considered Gay Taylor to be one of the twentieth century's important spiritual commentators, as well as an authentic mystic who experienced God's love by and through infused contemplation.

Reading Gay Taylor's unpublished letters, I found the following: 'Perhaps I had better keep the strangest part of my life entirely to myself. The thing of surviving and overcoming suffering may be of some use to others – I did mean that book (*A Prison, A Paradise*) for the despairing.'[5]

I take the 'despairing' to include not only the despairing and those tempted to suicide, but also those who suffer from depression, as had Gay Taylor. I also believe she meant spiritual people who experienced what St John of the Cross calls 'the dark night of the soul' – a state of soul very much like despair.

Let us now go back to 1958. In the 'Saturday Book Column' of the *Daily Mail*, Kenneth Allsop's lead book review appeared: 'Who is this woman who tells her tragic love?' He writes:

> *A Prison, A Paradise*, one of the most moving and emotionally searing personal confessions I

have ever read, unique in the remorseless honesty with which it reveals the inner life of a
woman enmeshed in an *Of Human Bondage*
relationship. This diary is a capsule social history of the sandal-shod romantics of the 20s,
the time of New Thought and rural artistic
communities of D. H. Lawrence and cottage
weaving and hand presses – of brave emanci-
pation and the bewildering loss of direction.
What does being in love mean? For Loran
Hurnscot it was sacred and profane love, light
and darkness.

At the time, Kenneth Allsop understood that *A
Prison, A Paradise* was indeed a *roman à clef*, but he
was not able to match the characters in Hurnscot's
book with real people. In fact, he did not even know
who Loran Hurnscot was never mind her husband
and her lover. But he was determined to find out. In
her archives I found a letter to Hurnscot from Allsop.
Because he did not know where Hurnscot lived,
Allsop posted his letter in care of Mrs C. Madge,
Girton College, Cambridge (Kathleen Raine's married name). He writes:

Dear Mrs. Taylor,

I am afraid I have to break the news to you
that I know that you are the author of 'A
Prison, A Paradise,' and that I also know that
your husband was Mr. Harold Taylor of the
Golden Cockerel Press and 'Barney' was A. E.
Coppard. I should add immediately that this
has come to my knowledge inadvertently, and
certainly not from any of your friends. I believe you have written a remarkable and in-

tensely truthful book, which I believe will become a classic of its kind.

Gay Taylor may have wanted to keep her life hidden, but it was not meant to be. After a while, however, the interest in her and in her masterpiece died down. She did receive, however, some glowing reviews, one of the best from the well-known writer Antonia White. She says:

> The friends who persuaded 'Loran Hurnscot' to publish these diaries deserve warm thanks. For this reader no personal record has been followed with such absorbed interest since Julien Green's Journals first began to appear twenty years ago. Julien Green began his diary in the hope that it would help him 'to see more clearly into himself', and Loran Hurnscot's purpose was the same. Moreover, she has done what the great novelist wished to do, but could not: 'write out my whole life in these pages with absolute frankness and precision'. There is no dichotomy between her 'life' and her 'work'; her life is her work, her subject, her medium, her instrument of discovery.[6]

I hope that in the near future, we will see new reviews of Gay Taylor's book. It is a book that has much to say to our present generation as well as generations to come. All we need is a publisher willing to reprint her remarkable book.

Indeed it is because Loran Hurnscot (Gay Taylor) is not well known and because her diaries, *A Prison, A Paradise*, are not readily available, I have decided to offer diary excerpts that chart her journey from despair to faith. One must keep in mind, however, that the spiritual journey is far from a straight linear line. It is rather a line with highs and lows, mountains of ecstasy and valleys of depression. Hurnscot yearns for the peace of the serene, straight line, but she learns, as all mystics do, that she is not in control but God, and the best way to travel on the spiritual journey is to turn everything over to God. Her words are far more eloquent than mine could ever be in describing her mystical journey:[7]

> And now and for many years to come, I looked on myself as a being with a broken mainspring, not whole nor able to have whole-hearted relationships any more. On the surface, I was willing to be amused. And the world was still very beautiful. But what I wanted was, death. (p. 167)

> Hellish weather, and I 'observe' that there is hell in my heart. Deprived of real emotions, I hate this doom of life with all my strength. I sometimes wonder why these years of life-loathing haven't produced an expression for themselves in the form of illness: why I'm still as sound as a bell. (p. 171)

> What am I looking for? What, after all, am I looking for? For God? No, that's too distant a goal. For a self that is fit to look for a God? (p. 177)

> I seem to have folded up my life and am sitting on the bundle, like a peasant at a way-side station, sullenly waiting, sullenly enduring. I've long ceased to want happiness – too frail and precarious a treasure to carry with

one in a world like this. It's better to be quite
cold and to value nothing. 'He who hopes for
nothing can never know despair.' (p. 183)

The present is being a sort of holiday, a holy
day. Life won't go on like it – it may be the best
that I shall ever know. There is a radiance
within. The screen my bitter 'outcast' pride put
between God and me has gone, and I know
both in spirit and (in a strange inexplicable
way) even in body that it is true that God is
love. (p. 201)

I went for a walk, then picked blackberries on
Periton Hill, in that far clump at the edge of
the downs. For a long time I sat out on the
crumbling turf, sheltered from the wind, with
the blue distances below, and warm sun lying
over this lovely autumn land. And suddenly I
was swept out of myself – knowing, knowing,
knowing, knowing. Feeling the love of God
burning through creation, and an ecstasy of
bliss pouring through my spirit and down into
every nerve. For it was ecstasy, that indissolu-
ble mingling of fire and light that the mystics
know. There was a scalding sun in my breast –
the 'kingdom of God within' – that rushed out
to that All-Beauty; its weak rays met those
encompassing ones and the bliss of heaven
filled me. (p. 201)

Real faith – even the smallest grain of it –
brings joy. (p. 202)

All this year I have felt myself deserted by
God. The blessed sense of the love of God has

entirely left me. I am utterly alone – weak and frightened and disgusted by life. When God leaves me I simply sink back into the worst parts of myself. Or is it that I sink back and therefore God leaves me? Pain and misery and starvation all over the world – and yet one believes at times that God is love. But I have lost the way to believe it. (p. 229)

Spiritual growth isn't consistent or continuous. The shape of the spiritual life is a tilted spiral. One labours, lumbers up the hard hard slope, there's a season of pure bliss, and in no time at all one is sliding down again. There one sits at the nadir, huddled and sulking and ashamed, for months or even years, pretending one is repenting but one isn't, one is just too disheartened and lazy to resume the climb. (p. 250)

I wish there were an Order simply for seclusion and prayer and contemplation, not these nun-lives packed full of vain repetitions but an experimental 'psychological' Order. Ah, but nothing is of importance except being at last back on deep prayer, once more in love with God. I try to be sober and careful, I time it so as not to imagine that ten perfect minutes are an hour – and then it makes me laugh, to think of timing anything to do with love, radiance, ecstasy. (p. 280)

Last night I was again in love with God. But now that the end of a golden thread is put into my hand again I must hold on to it, even at the times when it becomes barbed wire or a meaningless piece of tow. I keep thinking of the monk who said he was in love with God 'all the time.' But they can't all feel like that, or the world would crowd the cloister. (p. 281)

Last night I had a crucial conversation with God. I told Him I had obeyed for fourteen years the instruction to remain with the goats, and just now I was heartily sick of the goats – they were too difficult for me and I'd like a change. I fancied that God eyed me with disapproval and said, 'If you call my goats difficult, wait till you see my sheep.' (p. 291)

This secret intermittent relation with God is an almost illicit thing, it could never be lopped into the Church's shape. Do I go on ringing, is a messenger sent to fetch me, or what happens? I don't know and I can't explain. The 'sinking too low for prayer' is a dull sorrow or even a dull indifference. The world shuts round me, a closed shop. And then, the other times, when I half-rise or am half-lifted into the true, radiant world that for a space seems to interpenetrate this. But it never comes through gritty effort, it comes in stillness. How can I explain, why it is that one cowers away from it for so much of the time? 'Lord, I am not worthy.' (pp. 299–300)

Lately I've known something that I can only call 'being summoned': the state of radiance has come looking for me and sweeps me away, so that I have to lay aside whatever I'm doing, and relax into one of the very high states of prayer, which always comes now from the 'heavenly heart.' And then I come back to ordinariness, aware of the immense gulf that I don't know how to bridge. Interrupted here by the very state I was writing about: a quiet blissful suffusion of the spirit with heavenly love, spiritual warmth, blessedness. (p. 306)

Last night one of the very rare Christian images came to me. This last living-earning journey away rather quenched me, and I've had to struggle up from a lower place than I've been in for some time. Sadly I was talking to God about how is it possible to love a thing so low? And suddenly, in the darkness and at a little distance in the air there appeared the image of the Cross and the dying Christ upon it, but small as though seen through the wrong end of a telescope, and I sensed the words: 'Did I not participate, through my death, in the very lowest sufferings of earth? It is never lowness that separates man from God.' And the love of God that I have known so often in prayer became also the love of Christ, who has always appeared such a stumbling-block to me because of Christians. (p. 310)

Twice last year I revisited H—, and the little church that is holy and lonely. I stayed with a paragon, a treasure among women, who is loved, admired and valued for miles around. 'When first you came here,' she said one day, 'I thought you were very religious. But now I know you better I'm not so sure. Or else it's a religion I don't know anything about. And I must admit that I dislike the very name of God.'

'Oh so do I,' I answered warmly. 'That's why I prefer to call Him the Eternal Darling, as the

Sufi mystics do.' Was there a dawning of a look of startled freedom in her eyes? (p. 320)

And now that this long task is ended, the Eternal Darling resumes his intimations, beginning with: 'My dear Loran, you have been having a love-affair with me quite a while now. Do you mean to tell me that you really didn't know I was there all the time?' (p. 320)

Since a chapter of this book is devoted to Thomas Merton, it may be interesting to read Hurnscot's four reviews of Merton's books from 1949 to 1959 under yet another pseudonym, Scorpio. At first, she was not greatly impressed by Merton's autobiography called *Elected Silence* (title chosen by Evelyn Waugh, from a poem by Gerard Manley Hopkins), but over the years one can see her opinion change.

Elected Silence: The Autobiography of Thomas Merton (*Hollis and Carter*). *Review, 19 August 1949.*

It will probably come as a surprise to most English people to learn that monasticism is undergoing a startling revival in the United States, as though materialism were breeding its own antidote. To judge by certain films and by the best selling career of an American autobiography, *Elected Silence*, many Protestants and even many agnostics have a comfortably sentimental feeling about the ancient faith. But in spite of the faults of rawness and naïveté that this book displays, one can respect its author for honesty of purpose and the courage to carry it out.

He seems to have been a half-baked but

sincere young man trying to be a tough guy, and bewildered by the number of contradictory influences which 'tried, at every turn to feed me poison.' He spends an Easter Retreat at the Trappist monastery at Gethsemani in Kentucky, fails to become a Franciscan, gets Biblical sorties, 'Behold, thou shalt be silent,' which 'practically floored' him, and finally becomes a Trappist monk studying for the priesthood.

His story is fascinatingly readable – perhaps too easily readable. Of Father Louis of Gethsemani one cannot speak. But is not Mr. Thomas Merton perhaps a little bit of a *vulgarisateur*?

The Ascent to Truth *by Thomas Merton* (Hollis and Carter). *Review, 4 January 1952.*

This study of the contemplative life, which is also a study of that great mystic, St. John of the Cross, is a far more mature work than the same author's somewhat garrulous autobiography, published in England under the title of *Elected Silence*. No reader can fail to be impressed by the absence, in *The Ascent to Truth*, of the raw and *jejune* element that at times so marred the earlier book.

The Sign of Jonas *by Thomas Merton* (Hollis and Carter).

He (Merton) has certain misgivings about American monasticism – a dangerous combination, he says. 'Our energy runs away with us. We go out to work like a college football team taking the field. We seem to think that

God will not be satisfied with a monastery that
does not behave in every way like a munitions
factory under wartime conditions.' He con-
veys an impression of the contemplative life
being lived under strange and noisy influences, to which he himself contributes at times,
as when he careens madly about the woods in
a borrowed jeep he does not know how to
drive, whooping, 'Mary, I love you.'

Indeed, in spite of his sincerity it is impossible not to feel embarrassed at times by the
spectacle of this Trappist monk living his clois-
tered life in the full glare of contemporary
publicity, and it is clear that Thomas Merton
sometimes shares our embarrassment. Here,
one feels, is a spirit that might benefit to the
full by the austerer atmosphere of a Carthu-
sian house, and one is led to speculate a little
dryly upon the intention in the minds of his
superiors.

A Secular Journal *by Thomas Merton* (*Hollis and
Carter*). *Review, 2 May 1959.*

The many people who have been interested
not only in that notable (though sometimes
irritating) best-seller, *Elected Silence,* but in later
writings of Fr. Merton, with their increasing
wisdom and dignity, will also find an especial
interest in his *Secular Journal,* written during
the period from 1939 to 1941, during which he
was trying to discover what his true vocation
was to be. He had not at that time believed
that he was destined for the contemplative life,
but imagined that he was to remain a writer
and nothing but a writer.

It can hardly go unnoticed, incidentally, that he seems to have a chip on the shoulder about England and the English: his 'momentary' conviction in May of 1940 that 'England is done for forever' was a little ill-timed, and a little graceless from one at his vantage-point of safety and comfort. However, he recognized that 'we are all guilty of this war,' and that Hitler could only thrive upon a condemnation that disregards our own guilt.

Notes

1 James Hillman, *Suicide and the Soul* (Dallas: Spring Publications Inc., 1964), p. 73.
2 Loran Hurnscot, *A Prison, A Paradise* (London: Victor Gollanz), p. 198.
3 Ibid., p. 198.
4 'Foreword' to Hurnscot, *A Prison, A Paradise*.
5 Unpublished letter, housed at Simmons College in Boston.
6 *New Statesman*, 1 November 1958.
7 The following extracts are all taken from Hurnscot, *A Prison, A Paradise*.

Questions for reflection

- Have I ever seriously considered suicide?
- If so, have I kept this a secret?
- Do I understand that if thoughts of suicide persist, I should seek counsel immediately?

- What can Hurnscot's life teach me about the spiritual journey?
- What can her life teach me about despair?
- What can she teach me about prayer?
- What do I admire about Hurnscot, the quality of hers that I would like to emulate?
- Do I have the courage to do what Hurnscot did, turn my life over to God?

10

Poet Jane Kenyon: Battling It Out with Melancholy

In *Modern Man in Search of a Soul* (Jung's use of 'man' is intended to be inclusive), Carl Jung devotes a chapter to the 'Psychology of Literature'. He understands the importance of the role of the artist in helping his fellow brothers and sisters live their lives. The artist (poet, painter, novelist, sculptor) is the explorer of the soul's depths; the artist is the opener of the gates of the unconscious. Thus, the artist is able to inspire us to embark on our own inner journey. Jung writes:

> The artist is not a person endowed with free will who seeks his own ends, but one who allows art to realize its purposes through him. As a human being he may have moods and a will and personal aims, but as an artist he is 'man' in a higher sense – he is 'collective man' – one who carries and shapes the unconscious, psychic life of mankind. To perform this difficult office it is sometimes necessary for him to sacrifice happiness and everything that makes life worth living for the ordinary human being.[1]

Let us now examine the life of one of these great artists. Jane Kenyon was born on 23 May 1947, in Ann Arbor, Michigan, to a staunchly Methodist fam-

ily. At an early age, her grandmother informed her
that 'the body is the temple of the Holy Ghost', a
comment that the poet never forgot, and one that, as
we shall see, she lived by.

She attended the University of Michigan where
she received her bachelor's (1970) and master's
degrees (1972). Here she met the established and
respected poet Donald Hall, whom she married in
1972. In 1975 they moved from Ann Arbor to Eagle
Pond, Hall's family farm in Wilmot, New Hamp-
shire, where Kenyon's poetic career blossomed. With
the example of her husband's disciplined work habits daily before her, she began to work diligently on
her own verse and, like Hall, remained a good part of
the day in her study honing her poems. Before her
death from leukemia in 1995, Kenyon had published
four volumes of verse: *From Room to Room* (1978), *The
Book of Quiet Hours* (1986), *Let Evening Come* (1990),
and *Constance* (1993). Her best-selling *Otherwise: New
and Selected Poems* appeared posthumously in 1996,
securing her place in the pantheon of late-twentieth-
century poets.

She attended with her husband the South Dan-
bury Christian Church (Hall's family had helped
establish the church). Jane recalled:

> Something unlooked for began to happen. Be-
> yond the social pleasures I took from church, I
> started to take comfort from the prayer of
> confession and the assurance of pardon. I was
> twenty-nine years old; by now it was clear to
> me that I wasn't a good person all the time. I
> was sometimes irritable, selfish, and slow to
> forgive. It eased my mind to acknowledge my
> failings and start over.[2]

Many of her poems are nature poems like those of
her contemporary Mary Oliver, although Kenyon's
poems possess a metaphysical dimension that is
more reminiscent of Emily Dickinson than Oliver.
Her other poems have a Dutch-like interiority (one of
her late poems is titled 'Dutch Interiors'); they concern barns, kitchens, country inns, studies, bed-
rooms. Then there are her touching poems that
address her psychic and physical illnesses.

In her essay 'Thoughts on the Gifts of Art', she
describes each of her poems as 'a state-of-the-soul
address'.[3] She also writes: 'Artists report on the inner
life, and the inner life distinguishes us from centipedes, although I may underestimate centipedes.'[4]
On first reading Kenyon, I remember thinking, 'Ah, a
modern poet unafraid to speak the world "soul" ', a
distinctly courageous act in our secular world, especially the literary world of poetry where so many
writers don't believe in transcendence.

As I travelled through her *Collected Poems*, I again
looked forward to reading *Constance*, now a favourite volume. It is her most Christian book, suffused
with a Vesper-like quiet and Vermeer-like light, a
book that reveals Kenyon's constant faith in both
God and art, buttressing her in her most trying trou-
bles: her husband's near fatal bout with cancer and
battling her arch foe, her bipolar condition finally
diagnosed correctly when she was 38 years old.

Constance is dedicated to her poet-husband whom
she affectionately calls her 'Perkins, for Perkins'.
Employing Psalm 139 as an epigraph, she offers an
overt clue about the contemplative nature of her
book. The psalm begins, 'O Lord, thou has searched
me', and in the following pages we find poetry that
announces Kenyon's belief that God will remain

with her even when 'darkness shall cover me', referring to her bouts of depression.

Some of *Constance*'s most moving verse concerns
her husband's illness with cancer, particularly
poems like 'Chrysanthemums' and 'Pharaoh'.
Kenyon's most revelatory poems address her
depression: 'Back', 'The Argument', 'Insomnia at the
Solstice', and, of course, the centrepiece of her book,
'Having It Out with Melancholy'. It is this poem that
I would like to address.

The word 'melancholy' is the nineteenth-century
word for depression, a word used by poets such as
John Keats and Samuel Taylor Coleridge. By
employing it, Kenyon protectively distances herself
from the clinical term 'depression'. Thus, it is
stripped of its multi-layered, forbidden masks and
its powerfully negative persuasion.

Her poem is divided into nine parts: an allusion to
the nine rings around Dante's *Inferno*. And anyone
who has suffered from depression knows it is a fore-
taste of hell. It also alludes to the Stations of the
Cross, but, instead of Christ's fourteen, we have
nine, the last being Kenyon's 'resurrection'.

In part one, 'From the Nursery', the poet offers a
brief autobiography of childhood. Like William
Blake, another lyricist who well understood that
children are not immune to suffering, Kenyon
admits that even as a small child she had been
acquainted with melancholy, which 'lay down/on
top of me, pressing/the bile of desolation into every
pore'. Even childish playthings like 'the yellow
wooden beads that slid and spun/along the spindle
of my crib' rendered her inexplicably sad. Her sadness made her feel alienated from everyone, including her mother, for the 'anti-urge, the mutilator of

souls' had already layed claim to her. Notice that she does not say mutilator of minds but of souls.

Part two is titled 'Bottles'. Melancholy's root may be spiritual, but the poet attacks it with modern science by ingesting chemically composed antide-pressants like 'Elavil, Ludiomil, Doxepin/Norpramin, Prozac, Lithium, Xanax'. She describes their sickening, sweet smell and one receives the distinct impression that, although the poet is ambivalent about these pills, she must take them for they indeed help her.

In part three, 'Suggestion from a Friend', she recalls a friend's saying, 'You wouldn't be so depressed/if you really believed in God.' Kenyon remembers this comment perhaps because it is cut-tingly unkind and accusatory. John H. Timmerman's exegesis is worth quoting. He writes:

> Common belief had it that one 'caught' de-pression because one had done something wrong, almost as if one deserved it … If that's the case, and if it's just a mood, why then, just snap out of it. But one can't, no more than one can 'snap out of' cancer, or diabetes, or a heart attack. That is one side of the cruelty of this stanza … The other side speaks to the over-whelming sense of distance from God that characterizes depression itself. It is not difficult for the depressive to accept this distance as fact; after all, characteristic of the illness are feelings of low esteem, worthlessness, and abandonment.[5]

In part four, 'Often', Kenyon records the effects of melancholy, how after dinner she often cannot wait to go to bed where sleep is the 'frail wicker coracle' carrying her to oblivion. She longs not for tender consolations or long walks with her husband but for the escape of unconsciousness.

Part five, 'Once there was a light', is an account of a mystical experience that Kenyon also described in an interview with journalist/writer Bill Moyers. Because it is beautiful, I quote both the poetic and narrated descriptions:

> Once, in my early thirties, I saw
> that I was a speck of light in the great
> River of light that undulates through time.
>
> I was floating with the whole
> Human family. We were all colors – those
> Who are living now, those who have died,
> Moments floated, completely calm,
> and I no longer hated having to exist.
>
> Like a crow who smells hot blood
> you came flying to pull me out
> Of the glowing steam
> 'I'll hold you up, I never let my dear
> ones drown!' After that, I wept for days.

In an interview, Kenyon told Bill Moyers:

> I really had a vision of that (referring to 'Once There Was a Light' from *Having it Out with Melancholy*) once. It was like a waking dream. My eyes were open, and I saw these rooms, this house, but in my mind's eye, or whatever language you can find to say these things. I also saw a great ribbon of light and every human life was suspended. There was no struggle. There was only this buoyant shim-

mering, undulating stream of light. I took my
place in this stream and after that my life
changed fundamentally. I relaxed into exist-
ence in a way that I never had before.[6]

It is clear that with her glimpse of eternity, Kenyon
had come to terms with her depression, permitting
herself to relax into life.

Section five, 'In and Out', is a charming account of
the importance of animals in our lives, their unconditional love mirroring God's love for us: 'The dog
searches until he finds me/upstairs, lies down with a
clatter/of elbows, puts his head on my foot', echoing
Psalm 139, 'O Lord, Thou has searched me …' And
the dog's breath, the in and out of it, 'saves my life',
breath that brings to mind the Holy Spirit, Kenyon's
admitted muse. (One also thinks of Francis Thompson's 'The Hound of Heaven'.)

Section seven, 'Pardon', is a gruesome description
of what it is like to be melancholy's captive. She
compares this foreign 'other' self to 'a piece of
burned meat/wears my clothes, speaks/in my voice,
dispatches obligations/haltingly, or not at all'. One
thinks of the soul's mystical journey that demands
purgatorial fire before the soul is worthy to enter
divine presence. Her melancholy, like a 'dark night
of the soul', is so severe that she again must turn to
antidepressants to move her from its darkness: 'We
move on to the monoamine/oxidase inhibitors. Day
and night/I feel as if I had drunk six cups/of coffee,
but the pain stops/abruptly.' When the fog-like melancholy lifts, Kenyon feels as if she has been par-
doned of a crime she had not committed, a feeling
similar in tone to what the mystic endures during
purgation, a penitential stage of the mystical journey
followed by illumination – a serene time when light

again returns and reality has taken on a new sheen, or in Blake's terminology, the windows of perception have been cleansed. At this stage, she is able to return to her marriage and friends, to enjoy the beauty of 'pink-fringed hollyhocks' and to return to her study, 'to my desk, books and chair'.

Again in an interview with Bill Moyers, Kenyon admits that although drugs indeed helped her with depression, there were times when 'spontaneous relief from depression' arrived without their use. She also credits her belief in God in helping her to face and to endure depression:

> My belief in God ... especially the idea that a believer is part of the body of Christ, has kept me from harming myself. When I really didn't want to be conscious, didn't want to be aware, was in so much pain that I didn't want to be awake or aware, I've thought to myself, 'If you injure yourself you're injuring the body of Christ, and Christ has been injured enough.'[7]

In part eight, 'Credo', Kenyon turns the theological credo, a declaration of fervent religious belief, upside down. Here 'Credo' is not a statement of belief in God and the tenets of the Church but one of belief in facts. Even in moments of tranquility created by 'pharmaceutical wonders', she knows the 'unholy ghost' of melancholy will return, she has no doubt, for it has ever been so.

She does not very much like this depressed self that will again visit and 'turn me into someone who can't/take the trouble to speak; someone/who can't sleep, or who does nothing/but sleep, or call/for an appointment for help.' She cannot stop its return, for it always hovers over her life like an 'unholy ghost'.

The concluding section, 'Wood Thrush', describes birdsong. She is 'High on Nardil and June light' when she awakens at four in the morning. She waits greedily 'for the first/notes of the wood thrush'. When the bird's spontaneous song arrives, she is 'overcome by ordinary contentment', not a Keatsian nightingale, whispering to her of 'easeful death', but rather one of 'easeful air'. This bird she has seen up close with 'its bright, unequivocal eye', calming her with both its beautiful song and with its presence. Like the bird's 'unequivocal eye', Kenyon's sight has been cleansed, allowing her again to see and enjoy life's beauty.

That beauty possesses the power to rejuvenate and to restore is well known. In an interview with David Bradt, Kenyon tells why poetry matters:

> It matters because it's beautiful. It matters because it tells the truth, the human truth about the complexity of life … Art embodies that complexity and makes it more understandable, less frightening, less bewildering. It matters because it is consolation in times of trouble. Even when a poem addresses a painful subject, it still manages to be consoling, somehow, if it's a good poem. Poetry has an unearthly ability to turn suffering into beauty.[8]

Kenyon never lets go of the omnipresent hope that God's spirit will communicate with her, this time conveyed through the wood thrush's song. In his book *Enjoying God's Beauty*, theologian John Navone says, 'God speaks to us in whatever deeply moves, motivates and inspires us.'[9]

Constance begins with Psalm 139 and ends with the optimistic lines of the stunningly serene poem

'Notes from the Other Side': 'God, as promised, proves/to be mercy clothed in light.' Finally, here is Jane Kenyon's commentary on *Constance*:

> I use a long portion of the 139th Psalm as a sort of epigraph to *Constance*. The psalmist says, darkness and light, it's all the same. It's all from God. It's all in God, through God, with God. There is no place I can go where Your love does not pursue me. The poems in this book are very dark, and many of them I can't read without weeping. I can't read many of them when I do poetry readings, but there is something in me that will not be snuffed out, even by this awful disease.[10]

Kenyon is without doubt a tremendously courageous woman, her verse a mirror of her courage. Her poem 'Having It Out with Melancholy' is an incandescent poem whose light helps us through our own darkness. She says poets do not write poems:

> Just for decoration. The other job the poet has is to console in the face of the inevitable disintegration of loss and death, all of the tough nothings we have to face as humans. We have the consolation of beauty, of one soul extending to another soul and saying, 'I've been there too.'[11]

Every poem Kenyon wrote was an act of faith. But it was also one of solidarity with her readers. We can almost hear her say, 'I've kept nothing back from you because you demand truth and honesty. And If you see yourself in my verse, and I believe you will, I pray that you find what you need to live your life.'

We can often find what helps us to live in literature, particularly in poetry. Catholic poet and critic Paul Mariani writes:

> The Christian imagination, informed by its deep Jewish roots, opens the possibility of another response to pain, another way of understanding human suffering. In this scenario suffering is not merely something to be endured because it cannot be avoided. Instead, it becomes the vehicle by which we encounter ourselves more fully. It means a humbling, a radical reassessment, a turning once again back to the metaphorical road from which we strayed. It means turning back to God.[12]

Jane Kenyon's poetry turns us back to God.

Notes

1 Carl Jung, *Modern Man in Search of a Soul* , trans. Cary Baynes (London: Routledge & Kegan Paul, 1933).
2 Jane Kenyon, *A Hundred White Daffodils* (St Paul: Graywolf, 1999), p. 68.
3 Ibid., p. 138.
4 Ibid., p. 138.
5 Ibid., p. 138.
6 John H. Timmerman, *Jane Kenyon: A Literary Life* (Grand Rapids, MI: Eerdmans, 2002), p. 200.
7 Kenyon, *White Daffodils*, p. 160.
8 Ibid., p. 175.
9 John Navone, *Enjoying God's Beauty* (Collegeville, MN: The Liturgical Press, 1999), p. 15.

10 Kenyon, *White Daffodils*, p. 166.
11 Ibid., pp. 183–4.
12 Paul Mariani, *God and the Imagination* (Athens: University of Georgia Press, 2002), p. 259.

Questions for reflection

- Have I sought a professional diagnosis of my depression, to be certain mine is not a bi-polar (as was Kenyon's) condition?
- Have I had it out with my 'melancholy'? Have I looked it full in the face and accepted its reality in my life?
- Even though I may suffer from depression, do I realise that I am still in control of my life? Have I devised my own survival kit?
- Have I informed my family and close friends about my depression?
- Friends and family can be a source of strength and inspiration; have I not only informed them but also turned to them in my need?
- Depression inspired Kenyon to turn to God and prayer. Have I too turned to God for assistance; have I prayed for his help?

11

Mother Teresa's Psychological and Spiritual Dark Night of the Soul

Mother Teresa (1910–97) was an Albanian woman, her real name being Gonxha Agnes Bojaxhiu. When the book *Mother Teresa, Come Be My Light: The Private Writings of the 'Saint of Calcutta'* was published, it caused an international sensation. Her writings (mostly letters) indicate that Mother Teresa for most of her adult life lived without any sense of the presence of God. She writes:

> There is no God in me when the pain of longing is so great. I just long and long for God – and then it is that I feel he does not want me. Sometimes I just hear my own heart cry out 'My God' and nothing else comes – the torture and pain I can't explain.[1]

This excerpt is one of the most remarkable soul descriptions in the annals of spiritual autobiography. Furthermore, it is heart-rending because Mother Teresa is an iconic woman known throughout the world, as loved and admired as Princess Diana (each served God in her unique way). Mother Teresa is famous for serving India's poorest of the poor. In recognition of her love for and service to the poor, she was awarded the Nobel Prize. What we will try to answer in this chapter is, how is it possible that a woman who had dedicated her life so completely to

God and his people could feel so totally abandoned
by him? Mother Teresa, of course, turned to her two
spiritual directors – Father Van Exem and the Archbishop of Calcutta, Ferdinand Perier SJ – to help her
understand her inner darkness.

From a young age Mother Teresa knew she had a
vocation to serve the poor. When she was 18, she
decided to become a nun, of the missionary order of
the Sisters of Loreto. On 26 September 1928, she left
home and travelled to Ireland to begin her formation. Only there for a short time, she began in 1929
her long five-week journey to Calcutta. From there
she went to Darjeeling to continue her formation. She
was then assigned to teach at St Mary's Bengali
Medium School for girls where she remained until
1948, the very year she left to found her own order of
nuns, the Missionaries of Charity.

Before establishing her order, Mother Teresa was a
highly successful teacher. In 1944, she was appointed
principal of St Mary's as well as de facto superior of
the Daughters of St Anne, the Bengali congregation
affiliated with Loreto. In 1946, when she was 36, her
life was to change for ever. She had gone on her
annual retreat at the Loreto convent in Darjeeling, a
town nestled in the foothills of the Himalayas some
four hundred miles from Calcutta. While travelling
on the train, Mother Teresa experienced a decisive
encounter with Christ. She received from Christ a
second calling: 'to satiate the thirst of Jesus by serving Him in the poorest of the poor'. Mother Teresa
considered this day, celebrated later as 'Inspiration
Day', to be the true beginning of the Missionaries of
Charity. Her inspiration is founded on the cry of
Christ from the cross: 'I thirst.' Thus, her order is
interlinked with cavalry, with Christ's suffering; she
likely meditated on Christ's passion many times

during her years as a nun, but the words 'I thirst' must have passionately moved her.

To understand the origin of Mother Teresa's almost incredible life plan, we need to know that her life was grounded upon three vows. She writes: 'From the age of five and a half when I received Him (Jesus) the love for souls has been within, it grew with the years until I came to India with the hope of saving many souls.'[2] The latter is more a spiritual gift than a vow, but it must be pondered: how young to be so in love with God that she already was willing at such a tender age to do anything for him. The second vow occurred in April of 1942. She writes: 'I made a vow to God, binding under mortal sin, to give God anything that He may ask, not to refuse Him anything.'[3] This vow was one of her greatest secrets about which no one knew except her confessor (and later the Archbishop of Calcutta).

A vow for an Albanian is life-binding. Their word *besa* means 'word of honour'. To give and not to keep one's word is the greatest dishonour. To keep one's word, one must be willing to give up one's life. Not to understand this aspect of Albanian life is not to understand Mother Teresa. When she was inspired to found her own order of sisters to help the poorest of the poor, she had no one to turn to except her spiritual directors. Both of them put her off. They would not give in to her pleading, deciding to wait to see if her calling were a true one, from God and not from her own pride. She did everything she could to persuade them; her letters to them were eloquently written in English. She answered perfectly their every question and quelled their every doubt, finally convincing them that her call was indeed from God. Archbishop Perier finally gave her his consent to begin her work in Calcutta. She would, however, be on her own. She would have to find her own monies, her own place to live and her own followers, not unusual, for many of the founders of our great Catholic religious orders began with nothing; consider the Franciscans (St Francis of Assisi) and the Society of Jesus (St Ignatius of Loyola).

God was present, however, and through his grace, she carried on. In Calcutta two brothers who owned a home offered her their third floor for her headquarters. For followers, 12 of Mother Teresa's former students offered to be among the first members of her order (her order was officially established by the Holy See through Archbishop Perier on 7 October 1950). These young volunteers caused Mother Teresa some unexpected trouble, for her own order accused her of luring girls away from the Sisters of Loreto. Such a misunderstanding was only one of the many problems Mother Teresa would have to face and solve during her years as head of the Missionaries of Charity. Her official letter to the Cardinal Prefect of the Sacred Congregation to obtain the Indult of Secularisation, thus freeing her from the vows that bound her to the Sisters of Loreto, was written on 7 February 1948. She succinctly identifies herself and her aims. She writes:

> I entered the Institute of the Blessed Virgin Mary in October 1928, took my first vows in 1931, my final profession in 1937 at Darjeeling. I have worked in India (Bengal) since 1931. I was born Albanian but resided with my parents in Yugoslavia. I want to gather other souls around me to do the same work and together to serve the poor in their humblest and most dejected and contempted members. There are millions who live in Indian cities and villages

> in ignorance of God and of Christ, in abomina-
> ble sinfulness. We shall bring them to Christ
> and Christ to them.[4]

On the surface this statement seems to be quite a
frank and hopeful desire of any holy nun or any
Catholic missionary. Yet in another letter, this one to
the Archbishop, Mother Teresa reveals a secret longing:

> Some time last year I told Father (Van Exem)
> about this and he told me that this should be
> put before you. I am not complaining, I only
> want to go all the way with Christ. I am not
> writing to you as to His Grace but to the father
> of my soul – for to you and from you I have
> not hidden anything.[5]

Her goal, as expressed to the Archbishop, was:

> I am longing with a painful longing to be all
> for God, to be holy in such a way that Jesus
> can live His life to the full in me. The more I
> want Him the less I am wanted. I want to love
> Him as He has not been loved and yet there is
> that separation – that terrible emptiness, that
> feeling of absence of God.[6]

Let us consider her longing. She longs to love God 'as
He has not been loved', an impossible goal. How can
she love God, Jesus for example, more than his own
mother Mary? How can she love Jesus more than the
Father? Knowing that she is a holy woman, we cannot say that her goal is one of hubris. But we can say
that Mother Teresa may have been inordinately
influenced by Christ's dictum, 'Be ye perfect as your

heavenly father is perfect.' She is obviously striving for perfection, that is, for sainthood. The Church has taught for generations, and still does, that the goal of our life is to become a saint here on earth. Many of our great modern spiritual teachers, including Thomas Merton and Henri Nouwen, learned early enough that such a goal is unrealistic. It is more realistic and healthy, both men taught, for us to be ourselves and leave sainthood to God. And then there is the absence of God. Why has God 'abandoned' her? Is he testing her? Is she experiencing the classic St John of the Cross 'dark night of the soul', a purification process all mystics must undergo to win union with God? Or has she herself set up a screen between herself and God? And finally, is it possible that she is a victim of depression?

Before we examine whether or not Mother Teresa could have suffered from depression, let us review the stages of the mystical journey. Evelyn Underhill, one of the twentieth century's foremost experts on mystical theology, lists five steps along the mystic way (worth mentioning again):

> Awakening to a sense of divine reality Purgation of self, when a person realizes its own imperfections. Illumination – an enhanced return of a sense of the divine order, after the Self has achieved its detachment from the world. Dark Night of the Soul – a purgative time when the soul feels it has been abandoned by God. It is a time of darkness and loneliness; it is sometimes described as a mystic death. It is the time when the mystic is stripped of the last rags of selfhood. Union – the soul and God become One.[7]

We can chart Mother Teresa's life according to the above stages. She is early awakened to God when she receives the Eucharist for the first time. She knows then her life's purpose: to care for the poor. Her purgative time is spent in deciding how she is to follow her awakening. At 18, she chooses to join a missionary order, the Sisters of Loreto. Then, as a nun, after a retreat to Darjeeling, she experiences on the train to Calcutta her illumination: she is to found a new order of nuns whose sole purpose is to serve the poorest of the poor.

Her journey thus far is clear-cut. She is a woman who knows what she is about. Then seemingly out of nowhere comes her dark night of the soul. She reveals it to her spiritual counsellors and she receives sound advice, particularly from her Archbishop, who writes:

> With regard to the feeling of loneliness, of abandonment, of not being wanted, of darkness of the soul, it is a state well known by spiritual writers and directors of conscience. This is willed by God in order to attach us to Him alone, an antidote to our external activities, and also, like any temptation, a way of keeping us humble in the midst of applauses, publicity, praises, appreciation, etc. and success. To feel that we are nothing, that we can do nothing is the realization of a fact.[8]

What he is essentially saying is that she has no choice in the matter. She must endure this dark night because it is God's will. We must keep in mind that only a handful of people were aware that Mother Teresa was suffering this dark night. To most people she seemed a happy, serene, optimistic and loving woman. She had learned early on that one of her reasons for becoming a nun was to be an apostle of joy to the world. She could not ever let the world see into her soul. Thus, she constructed what Jung describes as a useful persona (mask) to present to the world. When photographers caught her face in repose, there was a great sadness evident. She surely had much to be sad about. Aside from her own personal spiritual problems, Mother Teresa saw daily the suffering of the starved, the ill, the lepers, the dying discarded into the gutters of Calcutta; she saw the newborn babies left to die on the piles of rubbish and garbage of Calcutta's streets. Why would not her face take on the tragedy of the human condition? Did this feeling affect her emotionally? It had to. Did it depress her? It must have.

To be depressed about our inhumanity to our fellow human beings is not anything of which to be ashamed. Mother Teresa surely, like most of us, had her bad days, when life gets to us, drags us down, makes us feel useless. We sometimes have no one to turn to. Mother Teresa always had God to turn to when she was young. Now he is seemingly gone, absent. He is not listening to her. She has to turn to someone, and she is fortunate to have three priests who know of her darkness and help her to endure it. We must also ask the ultimate question, 'Had she ever despaired?' Her writings indicate that she might have felt herself at the brink of despair, but because of her certitude that what she was doing in her life, helping the poorest of the poor, was God's will, she never succumbed to despair. And besides her certitude, there was also her blind trust in God, which sustained her through her whole life. To read Mother Teresa's letters and other writings, one cannot help thinking of the Jesuit poet Gerard Manley

Hopkins. His 'terrible sonnets' describe poetically the hell that Mother Teresa had to endure. He too felt that God had abandoned him, had not listened to his prayers, had not answered them, had not given him any thought. He felt that he was useless, his poetry worthless, his work as a priest a failure. Like Mother Teresa he put on a happy face, let no one see the darkness within which he abided. There were only two things he could do: pray and be patient.

There were times, however, when Mother Teresa came close to giving up. She wrote to her spiritual counsellor: 'Tell me, Father, why is there so much pain and darkness in my soul? Sometimes I find myself saying "I can't bear it any longer" with the same breath I say "I am sorry, do with me what you wish." '9

In 1959, Mother Teresa finally told Archbishop Perier about her 1942 vow, binding under mortal sin: 'Not to refuse Him anything.' She explains that she has always wanted one thing in life: to do the will of God. At the end of her letter, she says, 'The only thing that keeps me on the surface – is obedience.' The Archbishop may have been displeased with her making a vow on her own without the advice of her spiritual director, and perhaps rightfully so. Is Mother Teresa reaching for perfection? Is she over-reaching? These two questions are valid to ask, but we can never come to a definitive answer. There are some who will criticise her for hubris. Christopher Hitchens has been a loud and virulent critic of Mother Teresa, and has suggested she is an ego-driven, crazed and proud woman. But thank goodness he is a lone voice crying in the desert. Most of the world is in awe of Mother Teresa. What she did for the poor and suffering, well, there are not sufficient words to describe the immensity of her gifts to humankind. But again, how heart-rending it is for us who love Mother Teresa to read her letter of 3 September 1959:

> In my heart there is no faith, no love, no trust; there is so much pain, the pain of longing, the pain of not being wanted. I want God with all the powers of my soul, and yet between us there is terrible separation. I didn't pray any longer – I utter words of community prayers, and try my utmost to get out of every word the sweetness it has to give. But my prayer of union is not there any longer. I no longer pray. My soul is not one with You, and yet when alone in the streets I talk to You for hours of my longing for You. How intimate are those words – and yet so empty, for they leave me far from You.[10]

Her description of her soulscape is painful to read. But there is a comment that causes one to sit up and pay attention: Mother Teresa says, 'my prayer of union is not there any longer'. The last stage of the mystical journey is union with God, when the self disappears into God. Here we have definite proof that Mother Teresa has experienced Union. Which renders it more agonising for her for she has known the bliss of spiritual marriage, and it has been taken away from her. The mystics have always used sexual imagery to explain their experiences, a practice that goes back to the Song of Solomon. Imagine a lover who has experienced the bliss of total union with her beloved; imagine their nights of love, the joy of conjugal love, the knowledge that someone loves you for who you are; your tender, loving acts returned in similar fashion by the beloved. All one can say is that one has found true love. Then imagine what it must be like if the beloved suddenly disappears: no longer near; no longer answering any requests; in fact, there is only prolonged silence and absence. This is just a glimpse of what Mother Teresa must have experienced as a bride of Christ.

At the same time, there was in India another holy Catholic: Father Bede Griffiths. He was a Benedictine monk who went to India to found an ashram. He was not a missionary in the sense that Mother Teresa was. He was more interested in a theological marriage of East and West, more concerned about the idea of enculturation and dialogue. He saw the value of India's religion, Hinduism, and he strove for a synthesis of the latter with Christianity.

When Father Griffiths founded his ashram, it attracted many people. He himself, like Mother Teresa, won a reputation for holiness. People said that just being near him made them still and peaceful. He was a great proponent of meditation. He writes:

> There are different ways of approaching transformation. For many people, I always say meditation is the way. They have to learn to sit quietly, and calm their body and their mind and then keep open to their inner self. We have to see beyond our body, beyond our mind. If one sits quietly he can discover that there is a deeper self, a deeper awareness. Some people find it simply looking around at nature: the trees, the birds, the sea, the river, or whatever. The key is to discover something beyond our body and beyond our ordinary rational, conventional mind, to discover that deep self, which then can grow. Take the example of a seed: It is waiting all the time. Once we dis-

cover that, we can grow and our life can be
transformed. The reason why many people do
not believe in God, or anything, is because
they are totally centred in their ego, this lim-
ited human separated self. The challenge is to
get out of that. Whether we call it God or not is
not very important. We can discover that there
is something beyond ourself, beyond this
present world as we understand it, where the
real meaning of life is found.[11]

Griffiths offered Catholicism to the people of India,
but not by trying to convert them. He offered it
through the way he lived; thus, he attracted many to
his ashram, particularly Indian women who had
entered Catholic religious orders. He writes:

Today there is still a very big problem in the
Church in India. There are many people, particularly sisters, who felt this call to contemplative life, and they want to live the ashram
style of life, with the freedom of the spirit, the
customs of India. Their religious congregations
are often open to it in many ways. They send
their sisters now to us for retreats and so on.
But it's very difficult to fit it into their constitu-
tions. They are not organized for this kind of
life, and so it becomes a real problem. Some
sisters have to leave their congregation in order to live a more authentic spiritual life.[12]

We mention Father Bede Griffiths because he too
dedicated his life to India as had Mother Teresa. He,
however, did not have to endure the long dark night
of the soul that Mother Teresa suffered. Griffiths was
not immune to the dark night of the soul. When he

was younger, he decided to spend a whole night in prayer. He knelt down on the floor and had to struggle against sleep. There was no clear light to his prayer, and the light of reason was gone. He struggled through the night until a vivid picture of Christ in the Garden of Gethsemani took hold of him. He writes:

> This was a real death experience. I think I got up in the morning about seven or eight o'clock. I didn't know what to do. I felt absolutely alone and helpless. Then I heard a voice, not external at all. Something intimated from within: 'You must go to a retreat,' and I am quite sure I did not know what a retreat was (Griffiths is a Catholic convert). I'd never been to one or heard of one at all. So I went to the Catholic church where I used to go and asked if there was such a thing as a retreat. The vicar told me that yes, there was one beginning that Day at Westminster House adjoining Westminster Abbey. It was given by the Cowley Fathers, and so I went.[13]

The retreat put him back on his feet. The world became alive to him, his body seemed to fill with light and to have lost its heaviness. He picked up a copy of *Dark Night of the Soul* by St John of the Cross and read, 'I will lead you by a way you do not know to the secret chamber of love.' He says: 'I felt that love, a total love, like a marriage. It was unimaginable how the depth of it simply overwhelmed me. I can only say it was a sort of breakthrough, and the whole place became alive. The crucifix on the wall became alive.[14]

We cannot know for sure why one holy person experiences a dark night for a short time and another for a very long time, until death even. We seem always to fall back on the maxim that God's ways are mysterious. Yes, they are. Thus, we cannot definitively say what exactly happened to Mother Teresa, why she was not granted God's presence and Bede Griffiths was. But the fact of the matter is that both people dedicated their lives to the people of India. They both reached many souls. They both had many trials and tribulations, but they never lost faith in God. God remained the lodestar of their lives; thus, neither was ever lost. God was directing them, showing them the way. And they did what holy people always do: they followed his direction.

Notes

1   *Mother Teresa, Come Be My Light: The Private Writings of the 'Saint of Calcutta'*, ed. with commentary Brian Kolodiejchuk MC (New York: Doubleday, 2007), p. 2.
2   Ibid., p. 15.
3   Ibid., p. 27.
4   Ibid., p. 116.
5   Ibid., p. 164.
6   Ibid., p. 164.
7   Evelyn Underhill, *Mysticism: A Study in the Nature and Development of Man's Spiritual Consciousness* (New York: Meridian, 1955).
8   *Mother Teresa, Come Be My Light*, p. 167.
9   Ibid., p. 189.
10 Ibid., p. 193.

11 *A Human Search: Bede Griffiths Reflects on His Life*, ed. John Swindells (Liguori: Triumph Books, 1997), p, 122.
12 Ibid., pp. 83–4.
13 Ibid., pp. 52–3.
14 Ibid., p. 53.

Questions for reflection

- Am I being unrealistic, like Mother Teresa, in seeking perfection?
- Do I understand that seeking perfection leads to frustration and often to self-loathing?
- Do I understand that the whole concept of perfection is one I should leave to God?
- What virtue of Mother Teresa's can I emulate?
- Have I followed Mother Teresa's example about keeping one's word (*besa*), not only to God but to my friends and family?
- Have I done my best to help the poor?
- Have I learned that God's greatest thirst is for souls to return to him? Have I, to my small degree, quenched that thirst?

Acknowledgements

The author would like to thank the following:

Sandra Walter for her encouragement and scrupulous editing; Will Parkes, the inspiration for this book, for his professionalism and encouragement; Brendan Walsh for introducing me to DLT; Helen Porter for her excellent editorial expertise.

The publisher would like to thank and acknowledge the following for kind permission to reproduce copyright material:

Continuum for excerpts from *The Journey through the Mid-Life Crisis* by Jane Polden; *Psychology and Religion* by Carl Jung; *Suicide and the Soul* by James Hillman.

Farrar, Straus and Giroux for excerpt from *Eliot's New Life* by Lyndall Gordon. Copyright © 1989 by Lyndall Gordon. Reprinted by permission of Farrar, Straus and Giroux, LLC.

Patrick Howell for extract from *Reducing the Storm to a Whisper* by Patrick Howell (Pine Orchard Press, 2001).

Inner City Books for extracts from *Jung Lexicon* by Daryl Sharp.

New Directions Publishing Corp for *New Seeds of Contemplation* by Thomas Merton, copyright © 1961 by The Abbey of Gethsamani, Inc.

Orion Books for material from *A Prison, a Paradise* by Loran Hurnscot (Victor Gollancz, 1959).

Oxford University Press for *Archetypal Patterns in Poetry* by Maud Bodkin (1934); used by permission of Oxford University Press.

Taylor & Francis Books for extracts from *The Adult Development of C G Jung* by J R Staude (Routledge & Kegan Paul, 1981).

Thames & Hudson for *An Illustrated Encyclopaedia of Traditional Symbols* by J C Cooper (Thames & Hudson 1978).

University of Georgia Press for *God and the Imagination* by Paul Mariani.

University Press of Mississippi for *Landscape as Symbol in the Poetry of T S Eliot* by Nancy Duvall Hargrove.

DARTON · LONGMAN + TODD

THE GOSPEL IN THE WILLOWS

Forty Meditations inspired by *The Wind in the Willows*

Leslie J Francis

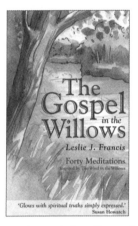

'Leslie Francis has achieved a most original and enchanting book by drawing out the wisdom embedded in Kenneth Grahame's classic, The Wind in the Willows, and weaving it into a profoundly Christian pattern which glows with spiritual truths simply expressed.'

'This journey along the river of life with Ratty and Mole is indeed a revelation – for Jesus Christ is their fellow-traveller in the meditations and prayers which Professor Francis has so skilfully crafted. To fuse the New Testament with an Edwardian novel in this way is not only to take a magnificently bold creative step but also to illustrate yet again that Jesus Christ is the same yesterday, today and forever.

'Read, savour, enjoy.'

Susan Howatch

The Gospel in the Willows comprises 40 daily readings and meditations which may be used through Lent or any other period of the year.

Order at **www.dltbooks.com**
or telephone
Norwich Books and Music on **01603 785925**
and **www.norwichbooksandmusic.co.uk**

DARTON · LONGMAN + TODD

LENT IS FOR LOVING

A Lent Course

Sheila Cassidy

Lent is for Loving is a beautiful new Lent Course by one of the UK's most loved Christian writers.

What is the point of Lent? If prayer and reading and self-denial are worth doing at this time of year, perhaps we should be doing them all the year round!

Christianity is not a blueprint for repression but for joy: for a life of fulfilment beyond our wildest dreams. Jesus said 'I have come that you may have life and have it to the full.'

In short chapters suitable for individual reading or group study, and questions for meditation and reflection, Sheila Cassidy considers the word 'LENT' as an acronym for what it really means to live as a Christian today:

L is for LOVE
E is for EMPATHY
N is quite simply for NO!
T is for THANK YOU GOD

Order at www.dltbooks.com
or telephone
Norwich Books and Music on 01603 785925
and www.norwichbooksandmusic.co.uk